Barry Green, a native Californian, served as Principal Bassist of the Cincinnati Symphony for twenty-eight years. As former Executive Director of the International Society of Bassists, he is currently directing a young bassist programme for the San Francisco Symphony Education Department, teaches privately at Stanley Intermediate in Lafayette and at the University of California, Santa Cruz, and has organized the Northern California Bass Club.

Principal Bassist with the California Symphony and the Sun Valley Idaho Summer Symphony and active as a bass soloist and teacher, Green has been performing for young audiences in schools in the Bay Area as well as bass workshops and in concerts on tour. He has studied with the legendary bassist François Rabbath and wrote *The Popular Bass Method* in three volumes in collaboration with Bay Ares jazz bassist Jeff Neighbor.

The Inner Game of Music has sold over 200,000 copies worldwide. Barry Green has also written seven *Inner Game of Music Workbooks* published by GIA Music for keyboard, voice, instrument and ensembles. His seminars, workshops and personal appearances sometimes include a unique lecture/concert called 'Journey into the Mind and Soul of the Musician' that demonstrates concepts in his *Inner Game of Music* and *The Mastery of Music* (also published by Macmillan). For information on Green's personal appearances and publications please contact his website at www.innergameofmusic.com.

Since the age of fifteen, W. Timothy Gallwey has been fascinated with the problem of how human beings interfere with their own ability to achieve and learn. His search for practical ways to overcome mental obstacles and establish maximum performance has led to a number of books on such diverse subjects as sports, management and work. He lives in Los Angeles.

Also by Barry Green

The Mastery of Music

THE
INNER GAME
OF MUSIC

BARRY GREEN with
W. TIMOTHY GALLWEY

PAN BOOKS

First published in the United States of America 1986 by
Doubleday & Company, Inc., New York

This edition published 1987 by Pan Books
an imprint of Pan Macmillan Ltd
Pan Macmillan, 20 New Wharf Road, London N1 9RR
Basingstoke and Oxford
Associated companies throughout the world
www.panmacmillan.com

ISBN 0 330 30017 2

26 25 24 23

A CIP catalogue record for this book is available from
the British Library.

Typeset by Parker Typesetters Service, Leicester
Printed and bound in Great Britain by
Mackays of Chatham plc, Chatham, Kent

Contents

Introduction
The Inner Game of Music

This is the first book written about the Inner Game principles of 'natural learning' that applies this methodology to a subject matter outside the area of sports. I am pleased that this should be the case for several reasons, since sports and music share similarities that are relevant within a learning context.

People 'play' sports and 'play' music, yet both involve hard work and discipline. Both are forms of self-expression which require a balance of spontaneity and structure, technique and inspiration. Both demand a degree of mastery over the human body, and yield immediately apparent results which can give timely feedback to the performer. Since both sports and music are commonly performed in front of an audience, they also provide an opportunity for sharing the enjoyment of excellence, as well as the experience of pressures, fears and the excitement of ego involvement.

The primary discovery of the Inner Game is that, especially in our culture of achievement-oriented activities, human beings significantly get in their own way. The point of the Inner Game of sports or music is always the same – to reduce mental interferences that inhibit the full expression of human potential. What this book offers is a way to acknowledge and overcome these obstacles in order to bring a new quality to the experience and learning of music.

I found that much of the self-interference in the practice of sports originated in the way they were taught. The Inner Game sports books presented a radically different approach to learning. Techniques for heightened performance were successfully conveyed, without the normal frustrations and

7

self-judgements that tend to take the joy out of learning and playing the game. In *The Inner Game of Music* Barry Green has translated these methods in a way that promises to bring new life and learning possibilities to this field of endeavour.

Since the success of *The Inner Game of Tennis* in the mid-seventies, many people have approached me to co-author Inner Game books on a variety of subjects. Barry was excited by the results he had achieved with *Inner Skiing*, and wanted to write a book applying the methodology to music. 'You know, Tim,' he exclaimed to me, 'I could write a book on the Inner Game of music, almost by just changing a few key words in any of your other books. It's all the same magic; it will work anywhere!'

I'd often thought about the possibility of cranking out simple 'translations' of the Inner Game into different fields. But I felt it was important for Inner Game methods to be re-created to reflect the unique and special aspects of a particular subject. I asked, 'Barry, how would you like to take two or three years and explore the possibilities that the Inner Game might bring to the field of music? Explore them in your playing with the symphony, and with your students, develop methods and new techniques, and then refine them when you have some experience in using them. Then, when there is sufficient evidence that the technology is feasible and workable, we might think about doing a book to share what we have learned with others.'

What distinguished Barry Green is that he accepted this challenge, and didn't speak to me about writing a book for nearly three years. During this time he did literally thousands of hours of research and experimentation with his own performances and in his teaching. Barry's commitment to making a difference in the way music is learned takes this book out of the realm of clever theory. It is a book that succeeds as a practical guide for improving the quality of music experience.

Barry wrote the text and developed the specific techniques that are presented. I consulted closely with Barry on the content of each chapter, and take responsibility for the integrity of the expression of Inner Game principles. Ours has been a close and yet informal collaboration. As Barry began developing applications to music, I became more and more intrigued with music myself. Not only did Barry and I lead Inner Game of Music seminars with groups such as the Music Educators National Conference, but I found time in my already overloaded work schedule to take up the alto recorder so that I might have my own Inner Game of music 'learning laboratory'.

What impressed me most about Barry was his ability to shift his sights from his initial interest in writing a book, to making the Inner Game of Music a breakthrough experience both for himself and his students. From this background of experience comes an unquenchable enthusiasm for what the Inner Game can bring to the music world. My strong recommendation to the reader is to experience this book in much the same way. This is not a book of 'right answers'. Rather, it is an exploration of new possibilities and a guide to be used in your own style of learning. It is an invitation to let go of some old 'rules', and to trust increasingly in your innate powers of learning. It is not a rejection of technique, but an approach to the learning of technique which does not inhibit musical expression.

My own brief experience with teaching these methods to music students suggests that they are remarkably successful. Musicians at all levels of experience demonstrated dramatic shifts in the quality of their music performance, even with brief instruction. I was used to seeing these kinds of transformations taking place on the tennis court, and got a special sort of pleasure in seeing such immediate results in music as well.

The same mechanism for heightened performance is at work in both sports and music, where overteaching or over-control can lead to fear and self-doubt. It is impossible really to concentrate on a tennis ball when your head is filled with scores of instructions. It is next to impossible to enjoy the game or play it very well when the emotions are involved in the fear of failure or not looking good before one's instructor. Fear and overcontrol do not produce the best tennis players; they are also likely to inhibit the production of good music.

It seems to me that the very essence of music is the expression of the self. It needs a milieu that is conducive to reaching into one's source of creativity and that allows for freedom of expression. Just as the end product of the study of music is enjoyment, virtuosity and inspiration, the actual process of learning and teaching can yield the same quality of experience. It is my hope that readers of *The Inner Game of Music* will use this wealth of material to help them experience the joy of music to the fullest.

W. Timothy Gallwey

1 The Mozart in us

Wolfgang Amadeus Mozart, of course, was a prodigy. How else can you explain someone who started to compose at the age of five; learned to play the harpsichord, violin and organ; toured Europe as a concert musician; and by the age of thirteen had written sonatas, symphonies, concertos and operettas?

But our 'serious' picture of the young genius may not help us to glimpse the very real child he also was. While touring England as a concert musician with Johann Christian Bach, he used to visit the taverns. Little Wolfgang and Johann Christian took a gleeful delight in playing with the brass spittoons, and while Johann Christian was content merely to score an accurate 'hit' in the centre of the spittoon, Wolfgang Amadeus would aim his spittle at the rim and send the spittoon spinning, until the reflected golden light of the many candles spun around and around the room, and everyone in the tavern began to dance.

Not too many people know that Mozart was also one of the finer billiards players in Europe, or that he gained inspiration for his music from listening to the click of the balls and the soft thud as they bounced off the green baize of the billiard table.

Was Mozart, as we so easily suppose, an extraordinary and special case? Or was he to some extent simply a child, with a child's natural enthusiasm, and a father who happened to encourage him in the pursuit of music?

Today we marvel at how effortlessly young children learn. Children who are brought up in other countries frequently absorb three or four languages, without confusing them.

11

Children who use the Suzuki approach learn to play music with enjoyment, competence and fearlessness.

Even if we view Mozart as an extraordinary exception, it is clear that all children have an incredible capacity to learn. As adults we may tend to play down their accomplishments by saying, 'Well, of course they can do it – they're kids! They don't know what they're doing.' But wouldn't it be marvelous if we could combine our knowledge and maturity with that childlike transparency and endless curiosity – so that we could learn, perform and listen to music with the openness of children?

Can you remember what you felt like when you were three or four years old? You may not recall the details of what you did, but your picture of your childhood will likely contain some memory of youthful enthusiasm, innocence or playfulness.

There was a time when nobody told us that playing was difficult, and we played music without feeling self-conscious about it. There were those moments when we marvelled at the excitement, the love and the sadness that live musicians could coax from their instruments. And there was a time when we first performed as members of a band, orchestra or chorus, and were overwhelmed by the massiveness of the sound, and our wonder at being part of fifty or a hundred voices all building to the same musical goal.

Even today, as listeners, performers and teachers, we still catch glimpses of that youthful potential within us. There are moments when we somehow play a phrase so well that we 'wonder where it came from'. Sometimes we feel as if we have learned a passage almost without trying; it seems to emerge magically from our fingertips. There are times during music lessons when we become utterly absorbed in discovering what makes a difficult passage work. And sometimes, at the concert, for no reason whatsoever, everything is somehow just right – the programme and the performance – and we feel caught up in the joy of a composer who lived and died a century or more before our time.

But why are these precious moments so few and far between? If we have the ability to listen, learn and play in this fuller, richer way, why do we do it so infrequently? Is it possible for us to recapture our 'youthful' ability to see, hear, feel and understand?

Playing the Inner Game

For years I heard musicians talking about Timothy Gallwey's Inner Game methods of teaching tennis, skiing and other sports. When his first book, *The Inner Game of Tennis*, came out, musicians were among the first to recognize that his techniques for overcoming self-consciousness and recapturing that youthful potential to learn could be applied in many areas – the playing of music among them.

But although I heard my friends discussing Gallwey's methods with the kind of enthusiasm they usually reserved for great composers and perhaps the occasional baseball star, the thought of using the Inner Game in my own life as a classical symphony double bass player and teacher never really clicked for me until I was introduced to Tim's methods on the ski slopes.

When I learn something new, I like to take lessons from an expert instructor who will tell me exactly what to do. I want to know what's best, and to perform correctly. But my brother approaches learning in quite a different style. He likes to teach himself. Jerry and I began an undeclared race to see which of us could learn to ski best and fastest.

Jerry was born with cerebral palsy and doesn't have complete control of the left side of his body. He never outclassed me in swimming – only in tennis, golf, academics and socially. He was an honour student and excelled at everything; I was a B student and played in the band.

My brother read Tim Gallwey's book *Inner Skiing*, and I took extensive (and expensive) 'how to' lessons from a ski school. A year later we met at a California ski resort. I was confident that I knew the correct positions for my body, my legs, the poles and my head. I had learned all the proper techniques for manoeuvring my skis. And yet I was amazed and frustrated to see Jerry skiing more naturally, faster, and with what seemed like an effortless command of technique.

I was scared to death. Here I was, right at the top of Squaw Valley. I was facing the same slope I had visited as a child, when I watched the giant slalom event there during the 1960 Winter Olympics. But this time *I* was on skis – and it was my first time away from the nursery slopes.

An endless stream of instructions ran through my head as we took off down the hill: 'Keep your weight forward . . . feel the inside edge of the ski . . . keep your shoulders forward . . . relax . . . don't fall . . . don't worry . . . don't stiffen up . . .' This constant stream of excellent advice did very little to help me get down the hill – and it certainly prevented me from taking any pleasure in skiing.

Jerry, on the other hand, had put it all together. He was relaxed, confident, his shoulders were forward, and he leaned easily into his turns, putting his weight on the inside edge of his ski as if it was the most natural thing in the world. I was still sceptical, of course, but it did seem that he had found a better way to learn. I asked him how he did it. 'Barry, it's easy,' he said. My brother knows just how to get to me. 'Just forget your instructions, feel the mountain with your skis, pay attention to what works – and read the *Inner Game!*'

I couldn't put off reading Gallwey's book any longer. I went out and bought a copy of *Inner Skiing*, and read it with a double purpose: to help my skiing, and to see how I could apply Inner Game techniques to the field of music.

It quickly became obvious that Tim Gallwey's Inner Game techniques could be applied across the board, in any area of human activity. The fundamental skills of *awareness, trust* and *will* provide ways to increase our concentration; to overcome nervousness, doubt and fear; and to help us come closer to our potential in almost any field. I saw very clearly how these skills could improve both the learning and the performance of music.

I began to experience with my bass students.

Early successes

The first signal that my attempts to translate the Inner Game really worked came when I used them to teach a bass player to relax his forearm. I applied one of the simple techniques that Tim teaches in *Inner Skiing* and asked Randy to pay attention to his forearm as he played, and monitor the tension on a scale from one to ten, with one representing a very relaxed state and ten representing a great deal of tension. We agreed to call his present level of tension a five, and I asked him deliberately to increase it to a seven and then relax back to a five.

Almost as if by accident, Randy found himself relaxing so much that he rated the tension a three. By noticing the difference in the way his muscles felt at seven and at three, he was able to recognize for the first time which muscles were getting in his way. He was then able to relax them consciously.

It seemed only a little short of miraculous. I had worked with Randy for months, trying to decrease the tension in his bowing arm without much success – and now he had managed to solve the entire problem without my telling him what to do! Better than that, the tone of his playing was now richer and more assured than before.

I began to understand how my brother had been able to learn to ski by himself. I saw the enormous power and effectiveness of Gallwey's simple techniques for entering a state where we learn, perform and enjoy ourselves to the fullest. I must have been pretty excited when I telephoned Tim that day back in 1980 and began a dialogue and a friendship that has continued ever since.

I wanted to explore and apply the Inner Game to music. Tim told me he was as enthusiastic as I was about the possibility. As we began to work together, we agreed on two conditions.

The first was that I should use only exercises and techniques that I had tried and tested in my own experience of music: if I wanted to use a technique that I found in *The Inner Game of Tennis*, such as telling people to 'watch the seams of the ball', I was to modify or adapt it until it worked in a

15

musical context, perhaps telling my students to 'notice the circular bow pattern during the fast even notes'.

The second condition was that I should maintain the simplicity and quality of the Inner Game approach. I was eager to set about translating the Inner Game into musical applications the next week, but I began to realize it is far from easy to create something simple. Five years later I am still refining, simplifying and discovering new techniques that utilize the three basic Inner Game skills of awareness, trust and will.

My work with Tim Gallwey took me from my home in Cincinnati to California, for tennis lessons and coaching in the Inner Game. It may sound strange that I learned more about music on the court from a tennis pro than in years of playing and teaching music, but in a sense it's no less than the truth.

Gallwey taught me that in everything we do, there are two games being played: the outer game, where we overcome obstacles outside ourselves to reach an outer goal – winning at tennis, playing well, or succeeding at whatever we are interested in – and an inner game, in which we overcome internal obstacles such as self-doubt and fear. These internal obstacles are the ones that interfere most with our performance, in music as much as on the tennis court, and keep us from experiencing our full potential. Players of the Inner Game find that when they focus on eliminating mental interference, their outer game performance automatically comes closer to their potential.

My experience of the Inner Game has brought me new skills and interests that I never dreamed of. Before I started to use Gallwey's approach, I played bass in orchestras, small ensembles and as a soloist. I also taught bass. The Inner Game has expanded my horizons to the point where I learned to lecture and conduct demonstrations and workshops. It has changed the way I practise, the way I listen to music, the way I teach, and the quality of my performance.

I now find myself coaching chamber music groups, church choirs, bands and orchestras. My work has brought me in contact with jazz musicians, music teachers, popular music buffs and dancers. And I have discovered, much to my embarrassment, that I sometimes give better piano lessons than bass lessons!

My entire attitude toward music has changed.

My playing and teaching used to be a little on the cautious and controlled side – and perhaps even a little boring. The Inner Game has helped me tap the courage and awareness to play more freely and with greater spontaneity.

I have learned to take risks and to attempt what would have seemed impossible to me a few short years ago. My teaching style has shifted from overinstructing my students to coaching them to learn from their own experience.

I have also become less preoccupied with my own 'serious' image as a classical musician. Where I used to structure my solo concerts around the standard double bass repertoire, I have recently branched out in ways that allow me to broaden the appeal of my instrument.

I now find myself working with composers, musicians, dancers and actors in a variety of styles ranging from baroque to jazz and folk. We have incorporated melodrama, space voyages and a visiting elephant (as 'guest artist') into our concerts. Together we have found new and exciting audiences of children and non-concert-goers to introduce to my noble partner, the double bass.

I have even been able to apply my new insights and communication skills in a more mundane fashion – helping my children with their homework, and improving their table manners. There are very few areas where the Inner Game can't be applied – with remarkable success!

Above all, I have recaptured that childlike sense that anything is possible.

About this book

We are all here to explore the Inner Game of Music: listeners and performers, students and music teachers, young violinists, flamenco guitarists, jazz buffs and professional musicians. Perhaps some of you have read other Inner Game books by Tim Gallwey and are interested to explore Inner Game principles as they apply to music.

What are you hoping to get out of the Inner Game?

Would you like to increase your appreciation for different styles of music? Will reading this book inspire you to take your instrument out of the closet, where it's been gathering dust for several years? Will it allow you to learn music more efficiently – and practise with more enjoyment? Or help you support your child through those difficult first music lessons? Is it going to help you play a better audition or recital? Will it help you 'shake the shakes'? Or do you just want to let out the Mozart in you – your natural creativity and genius: the composer, the child at play, the spontaneous and musical you?

Learning from your own experience is the very essence of the Inner Game. To help you do this, there are numerous exercises scattered throughout the book. Clearly, these exercises can't always represent every style of music from bluegrass to Beethoven, nor every level of musical accomplishment from the student's who's just starting to the virtuoso's. But we aren't here to learn an instrument; we're here to explore the possibilities of the Inner Game and the discovery of our own potential – a potential that can be expressed musically, in sports, and in a thousand other ways.

I really want to encourage you to do these exercises and play the Inner Game of Music with me as you make your way through the book: your practical experience of what I am talking about will teach you much more than a reading of my words ever can.

Some of these exercises involve reading music, but the majority don't. Some can be done in your imagination, and others need your active participation. I'd like you to feel free to apply the exercises at your own level, and in terms of the musical style that you feel most comfortable with: its OK to substitute the music that you are already playing for the examples I have given or to simplify an exercise that seems too difficult. One way to make a difficult exercise easy is to slow it down. By all means, the exercises should not become an additional obstacle to gain an experience of the techniques discussed. Many of my students found it helpful to do some of the exercises away from their primary instrument. For example, the singers can play some of the music on the keyboard. The keyboard players and other instrumentalists can vocalize either in their imagination or aloud. If you prefer reading the text and just playing through the music in your head, feel free to do so. The music suggested is only a guide or example of a way to gain familiarity with the concepts presented. The most appropriate examples of your own music may not occur to you until weeks or months after you leave a particular chapter.

This book is also designed to help those who listen to music but neither sing nor play an instrument – the music lovers without whom the rest of us would lack an audience. Although one chapter of this book deals specifically with the concert-goer, listening skills are discussed throughout the book and are an essential part of the Inner Game of Music.

The performer, after all, can only play what he hears, and so this book is as much about listening as it is about playing.

Overview of the book

In the next two chapters we shall take a look at the Inner Game itself, learn its basic theories, define some terms and see when and how it is played. In Chapters 4 to 7, we shall be developing the basic Inner Game skills of awareness, will and trust. Chapters 8, 9 and 10 apply these skills to the areas of successful performance, musical experience and learning and teaching. Chapters 11 to 14 speak directly to the listener, the coach or music parent and the ensemble player. The final chapter explores the application of the Inner Game to improvisation and creativity, and suggests some further avenues of approach to the incredible potential that exists within each one of us.

This book can be read in a number of ways. For some it may be an intense workshop and does not need to be consumed at one time. After the first seven chapters, the remaining chapters will have varying degrees of interest to readers from different backgrounds. I encourage you to read this book at your own pace and in your own way. Regardless of how you read it, I hope you will have fun with it.

Finally, I would like to invite you to send me any responses, stories and comments that occur to you while you are reading this book or playing the Inner Game – in your music or in your life. There is always more for us to learn, and I would very much enjoy learning from your experiences. In many ways a book is like a conversation, and when one person gets to do all the talking, it just isn't as much fun.

Pull up a chair. Reach for the music. And let's go.

2 The Inner Game

What is the Inner Game?

What is it that a tennis pro discovers on the court, that he is then able to teach to ski instructors and golf pros, business executives and telephone switchboard operators; that can help physicians design more effective programmes for the prevention of stroke and heart disease and help musicians play with more assurance, musicality and delight? What exactly is the 'inner' game that these very different areas of human performance all have in common?

Over the course of the next two chapters we will take a look at the Inner Game, explore its basic principles, and discover when and how it is played.

The two games

Whether you are playing tennis, engaged in business, or making music, each activity has its own challenges and ways to overcome them. It is, if you like, a game.

This game, the 'outer' game, is the one we all know we are playing. You play it in the 'outside' world, against 'outside' opponents. The context or arena is the tennis court, the office or the concert hall. The obstacles are your opponent's back hand, the cut-throat competition or the intricate fingering. Your goal is to win the point, or land the contract or play that difficult passage. And there are many books on the market designed to teach you how to play it better.

The fundamental insight of Tim Gallwey's approach is that you are also playing a second, or 'inner', game all the time you are playing the 'outer' game. This second game is subtler, less easily noticed and more quickly forgotten. It is played out in the arena of your mind. The obstacles are mental obstacles, such as lapses of concentration, nervousness and self-doubt. Your goal is to express your potential to the fullest. And very few books talk about it.

These two games, the inner and the outer, are closely interrelated – and each one has a considerable impact on the other. It simply isn't possible to engage in any human activity without playing both games. The problem arises when we are playing both games but think we are only playing the outer game. These are the times when, as Tim puts it, 'the game ends up playing the person', rather than the other way around.

In this book we shall concentrate on playing the Inner Game of Music, and leave instructions on the outer game – proper hand position, breath support, bowing techniques and 'the only right way to play Brahms' – to others. We will be asking you to let go of your outer game concerns and to concentrate on developing your Inner Game.

There are two reasons for this. First, success in the Inner Game is very often the deciding factor between success in your outer game and failure. Second, the Inner Game is a fascinating game in its own right – and the only game that can be 'applied' to all other games.

Tim Gallwey points out that 'we are playing the Inner Game every day, whether we're aware of it or not, and winning or losing it every moment.'

In a sense, the Inner Game is the key to success in the larger game of life.

We all carry within us a reservoir of potential, which consists of natural abilities, capacities and knowledge. We develop this potential when we face situations that challenge us to perform at new heights of achievement in any field of endeavour.

To meet these challenges, we have to solve problems in the real world around us. We have to play the outer game. You may, for instance, need to find ways to get the 'cool' sound of Miles Davis when it's your turn to solo in a jazz combo.

But there are a whole set of inner problems that we also face and which directly affect our outer performance. You may feel nervous when the spotlight is on you, or feel doubtful that you can pull off a difficult progression. These doubts are the challenges you face in the Inner Game.

As we turn to examine the inner world, with its teeming doubts and hopes and expectations, we need to know just what is going on inside us.

Inhibiting attitudes and tendencies – such as anxiety, fear of failure and self-doubt – make us feel stressful, and our muscles respond by tightening up. They also distract and scatter our attention and make us lose interest in what we are doing. In Inner Game terms, the kind of mental static that interferes with our natural ability is known as 'self-interference'.

Tim Gallwey's Inner Game approach teaches the awareness of attitudes that inhibit the expression of our full performance potential.

Inner game basics 1: the performance equation

The basic truth is that our performance of any task depends as much on the extent to which we interfere with our abilities as it does on those abilities themselves. This can be expressed as a formula:

$$P = p - i$$

In this equation P refers to Performance, which we define as the result you achieve – what you actually wind up feeling, achieving, and learning. Similarly, p stands for potential, defined as your innate ability – what you are naturally capable of. And i means interference – your capacity to get in your own way.

Improving performance by reducing interference

Most people try to improve their performance (P) by increasing their potential (p) through practising and learning new skills.

The Inner Game approach, on the other hand, is to reduce interference (*i*) at the same time that potential (*p*) is being trained – and the result is that our actual performance comes closer to our true potential.

The stumbling block: self-interference

Remember the worst moment?

I'd like you to go back for a moment and take a look at the most painful and unpleasant musical experience you ever had. Even if it happened years ago, you may still have a very vivid picture of what happened – the tension in your body, and even the conflicts that were taking place in your head. It is likely to be an event that is engraved in your memory with surprising clarity, and you can probably describe it easily.

I remember only too clearly the day I played the bass for a final in my first year at Indiana University. It was a juried exam and in addition to my own bass teacher, Murray Grodner, the examining board included the distinguished concert cellist Janos Starker; Josef Gingold, the dean of violin teachers; and William Primrose, perhaps the greatest viola player of all time.

I was a nervous wreck. I felt sick to my stomach and was certain I would forget the music I had taken such pains to learn. Playing in front of the acknowledged masters in one's field is hardly the sort of thing that's conducive to self-confidence and ease. My hands were sweaty, my knees wobbled (which is a problem when you're holding a double bass), my heart was pounding, and I had trouble just breathing comfortably.

Worse, I can still hear the little voice in my head, pounding away at my last reserves of self-confidence. 'I'm playing out of tune. What will they think? And I hit a wrong note there. Oh no, my bow is shaking. When will it stop? Still shaking. This is terrible. Now for the tricky part. Damn, if I could go over that bar again, I'm sure I could play it more smoothly.

Hand up, remember, elbow firm, relax the third finger and vibrate fast! Yippee, I got it! Hope at least they were impressed with that little flourish. . .'

I played as well as I could, given the battle that was going on inside me. And I don't suppose you'll be too surprised if I tell you the distinguished panel wasn't very impressed.

Remember the best

And then there's the best musical experience you ever had. Can you remember it? It may have been a lesson, a recital or a concert. What was it like? How much can you recall about the thoughts you had while you were playing? What was going on in your mind?

Did your mind interrupt in the middle of your playing to say, 'Wow, this is really wonderful – I'm not making any mistakes?' Or is it possible that you were so involved in what you were doing that your mind wasn't able to comment on it? And if it did comment, just once maybe, to congratulate you, didn't it almost make you lose your stride?

The hundreds of musicians that I have spoken with – soloists, orchestral players, young students and seasoned sessions men – almost all find it very difficult to remember much about the times when everything went well. They were aware that things were falling into place, and they remember feeling exhilarated and delighted.

That effortless fast technical passage, that quick motion to a high note when you hit it right on the button, and most of all, that unique suspended moment when you actually became the emotional or sensory quality of the music – the colours, the water, the love – we have all had times like these. They happen when we are mentally alert and aware, but too absorbed in the moment to be running any mental gossip. And as a result, it's very difficult to recall just exactly what was going on in our minds at the time.

The lesson

What can we learn from all this?

Most of us have very clear memories of that self-critical

25

internal conversation running on in our heads while we were playing poorly, and yet it often seems that we hardly remember noticing it at all while we were playing well. Isn't it reasonable to think that our performance would improve tremendously if we could eliminate that critical voice altogether?

Exercise: identifying self-interference

Take a moment to think about the things that make you nervous. Imagine yourself going on stage to play a concert and feeling those last-minute anxieties. Make a list of all the things that worry you, and then compare your list with the list I have compiled from literally hundreds of interviews with all sorts of musicians.

The musicians I spoke with, many of whom are at the top of their profession, all seemed to find themselves facing some of the same worries. Of course, the list varied from individual to individual – but the general focus was always the same. They said they

> doubted their own ability
> were afraid they would lose control
> felt they hadn't practised enough
> were concerned they wouldn't see or hear properly
> were worried about their accompanist
> thought their equipment might malfunction
> worried about losing their place in the music
> doubted the audience would like their playing
> feared they would forget what they had memorized so well
> or feared that even if everything went well, their parents would still be disappointed they hadn't gone into business.

Exercise: noticing the effects of interference

These doubts and fears crop up, in one form or another, for almost all of us, and not just in the realm of music. Business executives, salespeople, artists and athletes all experience equivalent doubts and fears.

Make a second list, this time of the mental and physical effects that doubt and anxiety have on you while you are performing, learning or listening to music. How can you tell that you are feeling nervous? What are the clues that tell you that you are not at your best? What is your body telling you? And what's going on in your mind at times like this?

Again, you can compare your own list with the one that I drew up after interviewing musicians of every stripe and shape. Here's how their answers broke down into our two categories:

Physical problems included

●   loss of breath
●   dry mouth
●   increased heartbeat
●   sweaty hands
●   shaking fingers, arms or knees
●   loss of the ability to see or hear clearly
●   loss of sensitivity in the fingers
●   tension
●   stiff body movement
●   feeling sick.

Mental problems included

●   inner voice's blaming or praising
●   forgetting the words or fingering
●   forgetting the music
●   losing the sense of timing
●   feeling distracted
●   losing concentration.

Once again, your own list will very likely include the same two categories of interference, and maybe even some of the same specific problems.

Inner Game basics 2: Self 1 and Self 2

If you think about it, the presence of that voice in your head implies that someone or something is talking (it calls itself 'I'), and someone or something else is doing the listening. Gallwey refers to the voice that's doing the talking as Self 1, and the person spoken to as Self 2.

Self 1 is our interference. It contains our concepts about how things should be, our judgements and associations. It is particularly fond of the words 'should' and 'shouldn't,' and often sees things in terms of what "could have been."

Self 2 is the vast reservoir of potential within each one of us. It contains our natural talents and abilities, and is a virtually unlimited resourse that we can tap and develop. Left to its own devices, it performs with gracefulness and ease.

A word about terminology

Many people, when they want to discuss these things, use terms like the 'subconscious', 'unconscious' and 'conscious' minds. They may talk about the difference between 'right brain' and 'left brain' thinking. They may distinguish between the 'reptilian' and 'mammalian' brains and the 'neocortex', or speak of the 'brain/body' or 'body/mind'.

Each of these terms and distinctions has its place and meaning, and in a later chapter we shall discuss the difference between right and left brain modes of musical activity. But life gets very tricky when people start throwing different definitions of these terms around.

These terms are designed to describe the ways in which the incredibly complex human being is 'wired and programmed'. They are technical terms, from the disciplines of neurophysiology, philosophy and psychology. As Karl Pribram, the distinguished neurophysiologist, has noted, we have as yet only the faintest inkling of what really goes on within the human brain.

Useful as these terms, they can only confuse the issue here. Self 1 and Self 2 should not be taken to mean 'left and right brain' or 'mind and body' or 'conscious and unconscious'.

They are terms that Tim Gallwey has coined to get around the complexity of these other definitions and the vast amount of argument surrounding them.

Unlike 'unconscious', 'left brain' and the rest, Self 1 and Self 2 do not pretend to describe particular mental structures or areas in the human body and brain. They describe mental and bodily processes in terms of their results rather than their nature. Hence the simplicity of Gallwey's definition:

 If it interferes with your potential, it's Self 1.
 If it expresses your potential, it's Self 2.

That's it. It's that simple. Self 2 may have access to the unconscious, or the right brain, or whatever; so might Self 1. The point is simply to know whether you are experiencing interference or expressing your fullest resources.

What are the characteristics of Self 1?

Self 1 gets in our way when it tells us what we should and shouldn't be doing, and talks to us largely in terms of the past and looming future. It loves to predict failures and successes, and often discusses things that have already happened in terms of the proverbial 'if only'. Like an after-dinner speaker, it also enjoys having our undivided attention.

Thinking is natural and thoughts are likely to be present in every aspect of our lives: sometimes we pay attention to our thoughts, and sometimes we ignore them and change the subject. Self 1 includes not only our own thoughts, but also whatever we have picked up from our teacher's instructions, the hints our friends give us, our parents' hopes and desires, and our own urge to fulfil or reject those expectations. It includes everything we 'think' we should be doing or worrying about.

While you are listening to Self 1's instructions, warnings, criticisms and general play-by-play commentary, it is next to impossible to pay full attention to the music. Even when the comments that Self 1 makes are valid and true in themselves, it keeps you from being fully absorbed in the moment.

It is helpful to notice your thoughts, and to find out how much they contribute to your activity and how much they

29

interfere with it. The best way to get to know your Self 1 is to give it a voice.

Exercise: getting acquainted with Self 1

While you are reading the next couple of paragraphs, I'd like you to notice any chatter that is going on in your head and then speak the chatter out loud. 'How am I expected to keep on reading and speak out loud at the same time?' 'My mind is pretty quiet today, isn't it?' 'I need to get to the shops before dinner.'

Notice how your talking interferes with your reading.

How many things can you pay attention to at the same time? Almost everyone can drive a car and talk, but can you read and talk simultaneously? If you can, is your reading as effective as it would be if you weren't talking? Do you understand as much, or do the words simply become a blur on the page?

That's enough.

Did you miss some of what you were reading? Do you need to go back and retrace your steps, rereading the passages you missed while you were thinking of something else?

Over the next few days, repeat this exercise while you are listening to music or playing your instrument. Notice how effective you are at what you are doing while you are speaking your thoughts out loud.

Even when you aren't speaking your thoughts out loud, they are still going on inside you. The distraction may be subtler, but it operates in much the same way, and speaking your thoughts aloud is one way of focusing in on it and seeing what impact it has. Most people find that their playing is less satisfactory when their minds are wandering or when they are listening to the 'talker' inside their own heads.

How did Self 1 get into the act?

Most children are avid and natural learners. For about the first eight years of our lives, we are in a wide-open state, ready and able to absorb whatever comes in front of us. We learn to walk and talk in the Self 2 way – without interference. Then, quite subtly, something changes. We begin to collect ideas, attitudes and concepts, to draw conclusions and to form our belief structures.

Of course, all this is proper and natural. These structures and attitudes provide us with the security of knowing what is known and can be taken for granted. But they also seal us off from Self 2, from the open and absorbing attitude with which we learned to walk and talk.

As we discover the value and utility of having relatively fixed ideas, attitudes and opinions, the gap between our 'critical' and ' creative' selves becomes wider, and our spontaneous ability to tap the resources of Self 2 gradually disappears.

The Inner Game is designed to help regain this natural ability.

What are the characteristics of Self 2?

George Leonard, the former senior editor of *Look* magazine and author of many bestselling books on education and personal transformation, describes what I understand as Self 2 knowledge in his book *The End of Sex*.

> The body is the best learning facility of all. It has thousands of feedback circuits. And the feedback is instantaneous. The body contains more information than all the libraries in the world, for it codifies, in its structure and its genes, evolutionary experience that goes all the way back to the first living organism. When we vacate our bodies [i.e. pay attention to Self 1 rather than Self 2] . . . this vast store of information is unavailable to us. When we reinhabit the body and learn to understand its messages, we gain access to a treasure of knowledge and guidance.

Self 2 has access both to our entire nervous system and the wealth of information that is stored in our past experiences, yet can be difficult for us to recall. Our Self 2, with its vast memory bank, contains all our past musical experience, everything we have ever heard, learned from others, or experienced for ourselves. It even contains knowledge that we assimilated directly from others without any specific instruction being given.

When we watch great artists perform (or for that matter our teachers and colleagues), we are continuously picking up and processing subtle bits of information. Have you ever noticed how your thinking or playing changes when you are surrounded by more advanced musicians? Are you influenced by their style of playing, their good judgement, their maturity and confidence?

What's more, since these great artists and teachers also learned in this way from other artists and their own teachers, what they pass on to us in this direct, non-verbal way includes a condensed awareness of the entire history of music. It is this type of non-verbal knowledge that helps us to develop our sense of what sounds, feels and looks right, and this sense of rightness in turn is stored away in less conscious layers of the mind and nervous system.

Brain researchers tell us that most of us only use a small percentage of our mental powers. The rest is stored away in our unconscious mind and in the body. It is the challenge of the Inner Game that we can learn to avoid our self-interference, tap into this wealth of knowledge, and so gain access to our full inner resources.

Self 2 performs best in an 'unthinking' state

My fourteen-year-old cousin Dana puts in her regular piano practice when she is in her most 'alert' state of mind – in the late morning or early afternoon. Yet she tells me she plays piano best when she has just rolled out of bed in the morning or when she is exhausted at the end of the day. She describes her playing in this state as 'relaxed' and 'flowing,' while her practice session is 'a struggle,' both mental and physical, with tension in her hands and arms and a galaxy of distracting thoughts – all of which makes her playing sluggish and unenthusiastic.

It seemed amazing to both of us that Dana was able to perform so much better when she was barely awake (or very relaxed indeed).

Other musicians, young and old, have also told me that

they perform best when they are relaxed, slightly ill, tired, or in a mood where they don't care whether they 'sound good' or not, perhaps while playing for a close friend. Somehow, lulling the alert, self-conscious Self 1 seems to play an important part in improving one's playing.

When Self 1 is disorganized, its interfering tendencies are kept to a minimum, and we gain easier access to the resources of Self 2. Our best performances often happen when we least expect them to, because we are allowing Self 2 to get on with playing, without our ideas of what 'should be' getting in the way.

Self 2, then, is an unthinking state, one in which we are relaxed yet aware, and are letting our true ability and musicality express itself, without trying to control and manipulate it.

Managing Self 1 and Self 2

It is understandable that our teachers, parents and friends may have instilled some fears and doubts in us when they told us what we 'should' be doing. As anyone who teaches the Inner Game quickly finds out, it requires effort and attention to teach without prescribing 'shoulds and shouldn'ts'.

The problem is that we have now internalized these instructions from our teachers and chosen to focus on them while we are playing. We need to realize that it is also possible to choose not to follow this kind of input. The critical Self 1 may tell us: 'You are going to goof up . . . Here comes the hard part . . . Relax your third finger and press the thumb . . .' But we don't have to listen.

When we eliminate our doubts and fears simply by ignoring the voice of Self 1 inside us, we also find we have eliminated its physical and mental effects. As our formula $(P=p-i)$ told us, when the interference is gone, our performance matches our potential.

Choosing to ignore the 'good advice' of Self 1

Self 1 is always trying to attract our attention away from the music we are playing or listening to. It is like a child who wants to interrupt a conversation we are having with a friend, or a stream of noisy traffic in the road outside the house.

What do you usually do when you are disturbed by the traffic outside the window or the children playing around the house? You may move to a quieter place, or speak louder, or perhaps pay closer attention to the person you are talking with. By focusing more closely on your conversation, you can often manage to 'tune out' the distracting noises.

The first step in coping with our Self 1 voice is to recognize that it may not just get up and go away. As it talks to us, we have a natural tendency to talk back – and then we are in double trouble. Not only is Self 1 talking to us, but our own response is getting in the way of our concentrating on the music.

We don't have to talk back to Self 1.

We can choose.

In fact, there are a wide variety of choices open to us. We can choose to focus on various aspects of the music. We can listen to the sounds, watch ourselves as we are playing, sense the way in which our body is involved in the making of music, or monitor our feelings. Whichever of these or a dozen other choices we make, we are consciously choosing to focus on something that is happening right now, in the present moment.

When we are present in this way (focusing on something that is happening right now), Self 2 has the opportunity to emerge and express itself.

Self 1 is like those monsters in the early video games like Pac-Man that rushed around swallowing up anything that moved. While we are performing, little monsters of mental interference keep on chasing us in a perpetual Pac-Man game, trying to catch our attention, determined to 'eat us up' before we accomplish our task – in this case, music.

In Pac-Man the objective is to clear all the dots out of a

maze; but we must also manage to avoid the monsters that want to eat us. A good Pac-Man player knows how important it is to be aware of the monsters at all times, but will also tell you that putting your full attention on avoiding the monsters is a fatal mistake: as soon as you concentrate on avoiding the monster closest to you, the others will creep up on you from another direction. If instead you remain focused on the overall field without going into a panic, and concentrate primarily on clearing the maze of dots, you will be more likely to outwit the monsters.

If we pay attention to Self 1 while we are playing or listening to music, the monsters of self-doubt and mental interference are liable to get us. We are likely to lose our place, our tone, and our sense of being in control of the music.

But we do have a choice.

We can tune in to our Self 1 doubts and fears, or we can turn away from them. We can choose instead to concentrate on the essential elements of the music, and ignore Self 1's attempts to get our attention.

Relaxed concentration

Inner Game techniques can reduce the effects of self-interference and guide us toward an ideal state of being. This state makes it easier for us to perform at our potential by rousing our interest, increasing our awareness and teaching us to discover and trust our built-in resources and abilities. It is a state in which we are alert, relaxed, responsive and focused. Gallwey refers to it as a state of 'relaxed concentration', and calls it the 'master skill' of the Inner Game.

Early in the development of the Inner Game, Tim Gallwey noticed that people played their best tennis when they were in this state. They were alert, yet at ease with themselves, and their attention seemed to be fully concentrated in the present moment. They enjoyed themselves, learned quickly, and seemed to be functioning at close to their full capacity.

In fact, this is a perfectly natural state of awareness in action. We all experience it often enough: when we lose track of time during a conversation with a friend, or when we forget we are watching a movie and get completely absorbed. Some people experience it while jogging, others in meditation, while typing, or even driving a car on the motorway.

We move quite naturally in and out of this absorbed state without giving it much thought, let alone thinking of it as 'a state of relaxed concentration'. And yet it is a special state, quite distinct from our normal waking consciousness.

Isaac Stern, one of the outstanding violinists of our time, sometimes plays very well – and sometimes plays superbly. His best performances allow us to glimpse his concentration, his power, his immersion in the music. It is as if he has gone beyond playing the violin, and taken us into his own deep experience of the music. We too are caught up in the same shift of consciousness as we give ourselves to the images and moods evoked by his playing. In Inner Game terms, we enter the state of relaxed concentration.

The challenge of the Inner Game is for you to bypass the critical interference of Self 1 and unleash the natural power and grace of Self 2.

3 The Inner Game skills

What does your Self 1 have to say about the Inner Game so far? Has it been talking to you? Have you heard that little voice saying things like ' It's true, mental interference does sometimes hold me back, but I just don't see how I can eliminate it?' Or 'Is the Inner Game going to tell me I don't need to practise?' Or even 'This all sounds a little bit too simple to be true. Where's the catch?'

Perhaps you have asked yourself other questions, such as 'What difference will all this make to the way I learn, play or enjoy music?' 'Will I see changes immediately?' 'Will it help me enjoy music that I don't understand as yet?' 'Will I be able to play music that has been too difficult for me up to now?'

Many of my orchestral colleagues and students have asked me these very questions, and their concern certainly makes a lot of sense. Sometimes people offer systems that promise a lot and deliver little or nothing. Sometimes complex subjects are simplified in ways that miss the point entirely. And sometimes we are led to expect rapid change in areas where our growth will naturally be gradual.

All this is true. Yet we often read in the sports, business or health sections of the newspaper about people who have managed to overcome their doubts and fears and have gone on to achieve conspicuous success.

This kind of news is intriguing to us because we instinctively recognize that our own doubts and fears are precisely the factors which are blocking our own success. We can take heart from the fact that these doubts and fears can be successfully overcome.

Any activity we undertake will bring us two kinds of result:

what we manage to achieve, and the way we feel while we are going about it. For most people the outer result is the one that counts: what we accomplish, whether we succeed, whether we win or lose. When you are playing the Inner Game, on the other hand, the quality of your experience comes to be as important as your actual success.

You are interested in how you feel while you are performing. Why? Is it simply because what you experience as you are playing has a lot to do with the amount of satisfaction you get from it? No, although that's an important part of it. Inner Game players are interested in paying close attention to their experience because it means they receive more feedback from their actions.

The opponent in this game is inside us. It is that part of our psychological make-up that creates imagined limitations, passes destructive judgements, and whittles away at our self-confidence – sometimes with an axe.

Overcoming your inner opponent means you experience a heightened ability to learn, increase your levels of performance and achievement, and probably enjoy what you are doing more as a result.

These results come about naturally, because when you are running less self-interference, you needn't be so busy fighting and punishing yourself. You are free to enjoy yourself more. You are more open to learning from the direct feedback of your experience, so your learning capacity increases. And you are more relaxed and have more energy to devote to achieving your goals.

Whether you win or lose in the outer game (and in tennis, at least, there is always a loser for every winner), the insights you receive in playing the Inner Game will turn out to be immediately applicable in other areas of your life.

Inner Game Basics 3: The P.E.L. Triangle

The three areas we have been looking at – performance (achievement), experience (including enjoyment) and learning – all complement and add to each other.

In goal-oriented activities such as sports, business or an audition, we commonly place all the importance on how well we succeed in terms of our outer goal – achievement. What we felt or learned in the course of that achievement is secondary, and we often don't attach much significance to it.

When the outer game goal of performance is balanced by the Inner Game goals of experience and learning, we are more likely to succeed in each of these three areas. We can picture these goals as forming a triangle – the P.E.L. triangle. It looks like this:

In order to reap the full benefits of anything we are doing, it is important for us to be aware of three things:

- the quality of our experience while we are doing it
- what we are learning as we do it
- how close we are coming to achieving our goals.

These three issues are very closely interrelated. When you pay more attention to how you feel as you are doing something, it heightens your sensitivity to the feedback you are receiving. This increased sensitivity helps you to learn more rapidly and allows you to adjust your performance to help you achieve your goal. The more successful you are at achieving what you set out to achieve, the more you will enjoy what you are doing.

On the other hand, when you neglect any one or more of the elements of the P.E.L. triangle, things tend to come unglued.

You may sometimes have performed a piece well while overlooking your own experience of your playing. Have you ever played a concert or recital for someone who gave you enthusiastic approval – even though you weren't enjoying your playing? You may have been miserably tense, and very likely didn't learn much that would help you next time around – either from your playing or from your friend's comments.

Perhaps you have sometimes focused on learning to such an extent that both performance and your experience suffered: you may remember overpractising some carefully planned fingering for a Mozart sonata, until the music sounded wooden and you came to hate the entire piece.

At other times you may have emphasized your experience of playing at cost to the accuracy of your performance. Have you sometimes had a great time getting together with your friends and pounding out all your favourite melodies – but without much regard for the timing or dynamics?

Each of these examples represents an imbalance in the P.E.L. triangle. And in each case your session will have been less than optimum.

Since they recognize the value of each of these three aspects of any task, players of the Inner Game set goals for themselves in each area. In later chapters we shall examine in detail how this is done. Designing a plan of action which includes goals in each of these areas – performance, experience and learning – creates a powerful impetus which can accelerate your growth as a musician and as a human being.

Inner Game Basics 4: Awareness, Will and Trust

Playing the Inner Game is a matter of developing three skills: awareness, will and trust. These skills in turn help us to achieve relaxed concentration, the 'master skill' that allows us to balance and heighten the P.E.L. triangle.

Awareness

Awareness is the first Inner Game skill and in many ways the most fundamental. When our perceptions are filtered through our ideas of right and wrong, good and bad, we seldom see as clearly as when we are in the non-judgemental state of pure awareness. That's why the jury at a trial is asked to keep an open mind while the prosecutor and defence lawyer both make their points: because premature judgement makes it hard for us to see things clearly.

When we are simply aware, without judgement, of the degree to which the outcome of our acts matches our intention, a natural learning takes place. That's the way we learned to walk, after all. But when our judgements come into play, we usually try to figure out 'what went wrong,' and then overcompensate for our errors. This often causes us to tighten our muscles and increase our overall body tension. We 'try' too hard, and this produces more errors the next time around.

Awareness, then, means simple awareness of what is happening, before the 'rush to judgement' takes place.

Will

Will is the second Inner Game skill. Tim Gallwey defines will as both the direction and the intensity of your intention. In other words, it is will that sets a goal, moves directly towards it, and then resets its sights to come closer to accomplishing the goal next time around.

Will works through trial and error. It uses the feedback that awareness gives to improve its aim. In musical terms, you make use of will skills to decide what you want to play and how to play it, and in gradually shaping your performance closer to the ideal.

Trust

Trust is the third of the Inner Game skills and it goes hand in hand with the other two. It takes trust to allow

41

simple awareness to take place, without immediately bombarding yourself with criticisms and judgements. It takes trust to explore the will's trial-and-error approach. Above all, it takes trust in our inner resources for us to tap into them and so perform our best.

Trust may sound like a hard quality to muster up. It isn't; your early successes at the Inner Game will bring you the confidence you need.

Balancing the Inner Game skills

The secret of playing the Inner Game is to develop these three skills and to balance them. As with performance, experience and learning, these three skills can be represented as a triangle: the A.W.T. triangle. It looks like this:

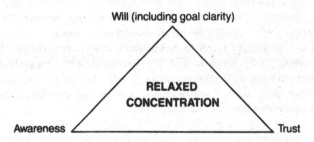

Each time you play the Inner Game, you will increase your skills a little more in each area. This in turn will result in improved outer game performance, heightened learning and greater enjoyment. A balance of all three skills will lead you into the state of relaxed concentration that we talked about earlier – and which we see in great athletes like Kareem Abdul-Jabbar and famous performers like Stéphane Grappelli.

We can choose relaxed concentration.

Instead of running through the usual routine of anxieties, insecurities and hopes before a concert or an important meeting, we can choose to play the Inner Game and use these three skills to bring us into a relaxed and concentrated state.

We are free of the grooves of habit that we were previously

stuck in, and find we are even more prepared for the challenge that awaits us – because we can adjust our actions immediately and flexibly in line with the feedback we receive.

It often happens that the Inner Game approach to a situation seems 'illogical' at first glance. In fact, the Inner Game suggests that we have had our values, and hence our logic, upside down in many ways. The exercises that follow explore a few of the apparent paradoxes of the Inner Game approach. They also offer you some immediate, practical applications of these three very fundamental skills.

Trying fails, awareness cures

Fritz Perls, the father of Gestalt psychology, coined the somewhat paradoxical phrase 'trying fails, awareness cures' to make the point that the harder we try, the more confused things often become, and that the remedy for 'trying too hard' is to be found in simple awareness.

Anyone who has tried to complete a jigsaw puzzle as the clock ticked on towards a deadline knows that the more they scramble to find the missing pieces, the harder it is to find them. As soon as the clock stops, on the other hand, the pieces virtually find themselves.

Why is it that we sometimes 'blank out' the names of people when the time comes to introduce them at a party, yet remember them perfectly clearly just as they introduce themselves? Why do the answers we missed in an exam so often occur to us as soon as we turn in the test?

The answer, surely, is that we are trying too hard. We are trying in an anxious or frustrated way, and not surprisingly, this makes us tense up. This kind of trying results from doubt. If we didn't doubt our ability to perform the task at hand, we wouldn't need to try. You don't 'try' to sit down and pick up the paper when you get home from work, do you?

It's the same way with music. Singing or playing a simple tune on your instrument is proably well within your capability. But if you had to do the same thing at Carnegie Hall in front of an audience of two and a half thousand people, you might begin to get self-conscious and doubt yourself. And then you'd really 'try'. It wouldn't feel anything like taking out your instrument and playing the melody in the easy security of your own home.

When we doubt ourselves in a given situation, whether the doubt comes from within ourselves or was instilled in us by others, we generally respond by 'trying harder' – with the result that we tense up and play less well than we might.

That little word 'trying' can often alert us to the fact that we are gritting our teeth, contorting our facial features and putting ourselves into muscular spasms in an attempt to improve our performance.

If we want to perform successfully at any type of activity, we need to keep Self 1 occupied, so that its tendency to doubt doesn't get a chance to bother us.

Exercise: Trying versus Awareness

Let's begin with some tabletop drumming. I'd like you to keep on reading and at the same time drum on the table (or any hard surface) with alternate hands, as rapidly as possible.

Fast

L. R. L. R. L. R. L. R.   *etc.*

Trying: Now *try* to keep the rhythm constant. You must keep your arms stiff, and alternate between the hands evenly so the left hand doesn't sound softer or louder than the right. Don't be nervous, even though I doubt you can do this as accurately as I have described. Really *try*. Grit your teeth, hold your breath, and hammer away as hard as you can. As you are drumming away, read this next paragraph (unless Self 1 is already dictating it in your ear):

> Don't get faster. Keep the rhythm exact and even. Uh-oh, do you notice one hand getting louder than the other? Fix it. Get it even. Don't get tired. This is pretty difficult! Just try harder to get it even . . .

How many times did you have to do it before you failed? Did 'giving yourself permission to fail' affect your performance? When you failed, did you have to work extra hard to insure failure? Did you notice any mental interference (instructions) when you finally failed? Was it harder to fail deliberately than to play correctly?

Most people, like Mary-Helen, find that if they 'allow themselves to fail', they don't fail. For some people, however, giving themselves permission is not enough: they still *try* to get it right – and wind up failing. If you recognize yourself to be one of these people, you may need stronger medicine. Order yourself to fluff it. Give yourself the serious job of getting it wrong, until your 'concern for getting it right' goes away. Like Mary-Helen, you'll probably find that when you stop trying, you start to succeed.

The reason is simple. You have released yourself from the fear of failure and are now able to focus your attention one hundred percent on making music.

Difficult tasks respond best to simple solutions

We have seen that *trying* allows doubt and anxiety to create interference patterns, blocks our natural awareness and produces tension in our body. When the task that we have set ourselves is easy, on the other hand, Self 1 has no room no doubt our ability to perform it, and this kind of overtrying doesn't take place.

Tim Gallwey refers to this approach as 'the Doctrine of the Easy'. When we are confronted with a difficult task, we can break it down into a series of patterns that are easy and familiar. Instead of dealing with the usual doubts and fears, we can then trust Self 2 to accomplish the task without interference.

Finding a simple task within a complex one and then accomplishing it can have remarkable results. I have discovered that students who have difficulty making a difficult bow stroke can manage it easily when I ask them to draw a circle in the air with their bow. Wind players find they can develop steady breath control by pretending to inflate a balloon through the mouthpiece of their instrument.

The trick is to get Self 1 off your back by making your task so simple that you sidestep its usual interference. Performing easy and relevant tasks that are similar to more complex movements allows students to execute new and complex tasks with confidence, tasks that might otherwise have required many hours of practice.

Exercise: Trust – easy and familiar

Jim, a marimba player, was finding it difficult to read all the notes in a fast piece accurately. The challenge was for him to find something *simple* and *relevant* in the music to focus on so he wouldn't have to concentrate on each note separately. Jim's solution was to notice the patterns formed by each group of four notes. He found that when he paid attention to these patterns, he could play his piece accurately without getting caught up in individual notes.

Play the notes in the phrase below, or sing them with a simple, open vowel sound like 'ta, ta, ta, ta'. Concentrate on reading every note, and read the passage as fast as possible.

(Play) Moderately fast

(Voice) Ta-ta-ta-ta *etc.*

Now repeat the same passage. This time don't concentrate on single notes, but follow the direction of the arrows, and focus on the patterns that each group of four notes creates.

Moderately fast

(Voice) ta ta *etc.*

When you're playing a difficult passage, ask yourself what can be simplified or unified. Put your concentration on this 'easy' unifying or simplifying element (the grouping of notes, a set of fingerings, string crossings, or whatever). And trust Self 2 to play 'automatically' the notes you are not focusing on directly.

By releasing conscious control of every note, and trusting Self 2 to perform, you will not only find how smoothly Self 2 is able to manage tasks that were difficult before. You will also be gaining confidence in Self 2 in ways that will later allow you to play extremely technical passages with an assurance and musical feeling that would otherwise seem impossible.

You have now learned the basics of the Inner Game and have begun to see them at work in your own music. Over the next four chapters we shall be exploring applications of the three Inner Game skills in more detail.

4 The power of awareness

While I was receiving my musical education, I searched anywhere and everywhere to find out what it is that really makes music come alive. I asked my teachers and friends for their theories. I read a small mountain of books. While most of the answers I received had something to teach me, none of them quite hit the spot.

When Tim Gallwey finally suggested that I should find out for myself by paying attention to my own experience, I was almost shocked. We have come to expect that authorities and teachers will supply us with their insights and their definitive answers to everything. And yet the answer we're looking for is often right under our nose all along.

As I began to use the various 'awareness skills' that Tim taught me, and to develop my own variations on them specifically relating to music, it became clear that my best teacher had been right there inside me all the time. Just as you never see your own face until you glimpse it in a mirror, so it often takes a nudge from someone else to draw your attention to the enormous reservoir of potential that you carry within you.

I found that awareness, the simple quality of attention that we can pay to events, people and things, works like a torch. It illuminates things that we were 'in the dark about', and shows us clearly things that we already almost knew. Yet we seldom really allow our awareness free rein to function.

Our awareness is greatest when all our faculties are working and we are paying attention to what's happening. It makes use of all our senses, taking its cues from what we see and imagine, hear and feel. Awareness shows us what feels and works best for us. As we shall see, it can even locate specific problem areas, discover solutions, increase our options and facilitate instant changes. Not only can awareness help us through technical musical challenges of many kinds, it can also enhance our ability to be swept up in the music, to become one with it.

Inner and outer distractions

You have probably noticed how distracting and upsetting it can be if you're watching a great movie and the person sitting next to you asks you a question like 'Wasn't she in *Revenge of the Barbershop Vampires*?' or ' Do you think he's the villian?' By the time you've answered, you may have missed an important clue, or the significant first glance between two lovers. Even if you're just looking at a beautiful sunset and someone says, 'Isn't it marvellous,' the effort of putting words on your feelings can be enough to frighten the feelings themselves away.

When we are playing a sonata or listening to an opera and a voice in our head keeps up a monologue about the quality of the playing, the same thing happens. Our attention wavers between the experience itself and the opinions we are forming about it. And that means we're distracted from the performance itself.

These two kinds of distraction – external and internal – are always cropping up, and it would be unrealistic to hope we could go through life without them. But there is a technique we can use to minimize their impact on us.

Choosing a focus for our awareness

Here's the strategy: by accepting distractions and then consciously choosing to focus our attention elsewhere, we can increase our awareness of the music – and lessen the amount of frustration we feel at the distractions.

In order to take real advantage of everything that simple awareness can teach us, we need to leave our assumptions and ready-made judgements on one side and pay attention to what is actually going on. We can choose to put our attention where we want instead of leaving it on the distractions.

What's important here is that we should choose a focus for our awareness in the present moment, something happening right now – and not wander off into the past or future. When we are aware of what's happening in the present moment, our concentration develops and things often seem to improve almost effortlessly.

As musicians and listeners we need to focus on the present moment, and that means knowing *where* to place our concentration (or attention): our sight, hearing, feelings and understanding. Let's look at each of these possibilities in turn.

1. Being present by paying attention to sight

The first time I flew in a small plane, we took off from Wellington, New Zealand, in heavy fog. As we climbed through the pea soup, the pilot ignored my repeated and somewhat worried questions about where we were and whether we were doing all right. He didn't answer; he didn't even nod or shake his head. He was glued to his instrument panel, occasionally talking on the radio, but seemingly not the least aware of my existence.

Finally, we broke through the fog, and after a few minutes the pilot removed the headphone from one ear, took his hands off the controls, put down his chart, and looked out the cabin window for the first time. The plane was flying on automatic pilot, and he was free to talk to me.

He apologized for not responding to me earlier, but assured me that if he had, we might not have been around to talk about it now. He explained that he'd been 'flying by the instruments' and that he couldn't afford to allow himself to be distracted by my chatter.

My pilot made me extremely aware of the importance of 'keeping an eye on the instruments'. The next time I noticed myself playing the bass with a thin tone, I looked down at my instrument – and noticed my bow was moving in the wrong place. I was able to restore the tone by adjusting the bowing. Simply 'watching your instrument' is one way to focus your awareness in the present moment by paying attention to sight.

Another way to do this is to watch the notes on the score. I've found that I can see each note and the complete phrase at the same time. This heightens my observation of the dynamic notations – the fortes, pianissimos and crescendos – and results in more expressive playing; and when I listen to music, it also heightens my appreciation.

I also use the sense of sight to focus my awareness in the present moment while playing pieces that I have memorized: I close my eyes and visualize the score, reading it as if it were there on the stand in front of me. I can also imagine the patterns my fingers are making as I play, without looking at them.

If you're distracted while you're listening to a concert or a record, watching the musicians or letting the music evoke images can bring you back into focus.

Exercise: Focusing on sight

Play some music, and when you find you are getting distracted or anxious, use the techniques of looking at your instrument or focusing on the score (visualizing it if you are playing from memory). If you are a listener, visualize the musicians who are playing the piece while you listen to it, or allow the feelings expressed by the music to evoke images and 'movies in your mind'.

What happened to the distractions? What did you notice about the quality of your attention? About your technique? About your instrument? About your playing? About your feelings? About the way you listen?

2. Being present by paying attention to sound

Just as we can choose to focus our awareness on sight, we can also use sound as a focus. I have found that listening with full awareness can silence the critical voice inside me, draw my attention more fully into the music, and help to relax my body when it is feeling jittery or tense.

Exercise: Focusing on sound

As you are reading this book, begin to focus on the sound you can hear in the environment around you. Do you hear any buzzes, scrapings, drones or whirring noises? Are there cars or trucks on the highway outside your house or practice room? Can you hear the purr of the refrigerator, or the high, ringing sound of lights, people talking or children playing, wind in the trees or rain against the window?

Now focus on only one sound – any sound. Is it steady? Is its volume steady? Does it have a rhythm to it? Does it change pitch? Is it a mixture of different pitches – some high and some low sounds? Stay with this sound for a few moments.

While you were focusing on this sound, did the other sounds in your environment tend to fade into the background?

Go to a jazz club or an opera – alone. Avoid the crowd, and focus your attention on the music, not the people around you. Listen to a new recording – alone. Don't do the crossword puzzle or clean the house: just listen to the many layers of sound, the way an auto mechanic listens to a car and then singles out the chirp in the water pump or whatever. Listen to music the way a veteran deer hunter listens to the sounds of the forest.

Focusing on the sound of your playing or the music you are listening to will help to reduce Self 1 small talk, and make you less likely to be distracted by other sounds in the environment. It will also help to decrease any physical stress you may be feeling and to relax your muscles. It will bring your attention into the present and give you important feedback about how you are playing.

3. Being present by paying attention to feelings

Our feelings are another possible focus of attention that will bring our awareness into the present moment. These include both the feelings that the music is intended to express and the feelings that we ourselves come up with. Our feelings are a very natural focus for our attention and can readily draw us out of our Self 1 preoccupations and distractions.

Exercise: Focusing on feelings

Find some music to play on your tape recorder, record player or radio. Listen for the feelings that the music expresses. Is it expressing love, anger, excitement, peace, happiness, sadness? Does it include a mixture of feelings?

Let yourself float into the feelings the music expresses. Let the music carry you away.

Notice how your body feels the music you are listening to. Where in your body do you feel the higher pitches? Where do you feel the lower vibrations? In your head, throat, fingers, arms, legs, stomach?

Now play or sing a piece of music. Again, notice the feelings the music expresses. Notice your own feelings as you are playing. Are they the same as the feelings expressed, or different? Don't judge or criticize yourself; simply be aware of your feelings.

Let yourself float a little more into the feelings expressed by the music. How does this affect your own feelings as you play?

Again, notice how your body feels the music you are playing or singing. Do the high notes register in your head? Where do you feel the low notes?

Identifying the emotional and physical components of feeling helps you to become interested and absorbed in the music and is yet another way to divert Self 1 'traffic'.

4. Being present by paying attention to what you know

Our knowledge of the music we play or hear goes far deeper than we sometimes realize. Our brain stores away all the experiences we have had from childhood on, including the music we have heard on the radio, in concerts and in our earliest music lessons. Although these memories are buried under more recent experiences, they can still influence us.

When you hear yourself saying 'I know this sounds wrong, but I can't put my finger on just why', you are acknowledging this kind of buried knowing. Pay attention to it and see how your playing imperceptibly shifts until you have it right.

We can also learn about the music we are playing by finding out about the composer and his or her intentions, the famous first performance, the ways in which the public received the work, and so on.

Focusing on our buried or learned knowledge of the music we are listening to or playing is another way to shake distraction and increase our absorption in the music itself.

I remember that Brian felt particularly nervous when he was asked to play Max Bruch's 'Kol Nidrei' for the class. He didn't know what the piece was about, so I explained that the music was an instrumental transcription of an ancient Hebrew chant sung at the most solemn holy day in the Jewish calendar – Yom Kippur, the Day of Atonement. I told him the Day of Atonement was a day of mourning, suffering and repentance, and asked Brian to allow the music to express some of these feelings. He forgot his anxiety and played 'Kol Nidrei' as an expression of intense pleading, a voice wrung from the heart.

Exercise: Focusing on What We Know

Over the next few days, read a little about the writing and first performance of a piece you would like to get to know better. As you are playing the piece (or listening to it), notice whether this knowledge has an effect on your appreciation and understanding of the music.

On Awareness

We have discovered that focusing our awareness on one element of the present moment is a simple way to direct our concentration, cope with mental and other distractions, and bring us closer to the music. Later we shall explore in greater detail how awareness can enhance our experience of music, our performance and our learning. But first, let's look a little more closely at awareness itself and the way it works.

In the last chapter we saw that awareness can function as an 'antidote to trying'. We noticed that the harder we tried, the worse things got. Yet when we're aware of what is happening in the present moment – through focusing on sight, sound, feeling or knowing – we relax out of our 'trying' attitude and allow positive changes to occur.

Awareness allows us to accept 'what is' without fighting it or trying to change it. We can see, hear, feel and know what works and what doesn't. This feedback, based as it is on what is actually happening, allows us to choose the most natural direction in which to change.

There are four ways in which awareness can bring about positive change:

1. Sometimes all that is required is to bring awareness to bear on the problem, which is then instantly recognized and 'cured'. When I asked Jane to notice if she was singing in pitch in the fourth bar, she instantly noticed that she was hitting her highest note a little sharp, and it immediately corrected itself.

2. At other times awareness gives us room to tolerate things the way they are, and then choose an alternative focus for our attention. Before every guitar recital, Jonathan feared that his hands would perspire – and, of course, they did. When I showed him that his sweaty fingers didn't really affect the quality of his music, he became less anxious and 'allowed' them to perspire. The problem gradually disappeared.

3. Awareness can allow us to notice subtle changes and thus gives us new tools with which we can solve problems. The decay of a piano tone is rather quick.

So it is difficult to sustain chords. Janice wanted a smooth connection on the chords of the Chopin C Minor Prelude. When she managed even a hint of the legato sound she needed, she noticed subtle changes in her playing. By gradually increasing these, she created the sustained effect she was looking for.

4. Lastly, awareness can sometimes let us see past the immediate problem to the 'problem behind the problem'. When Alice was having problems with an intricate bowing stroke, her awareness showed her that her real problem was with the other hand, which was not in the right place.

Let's see how these four ways in which awareness can work for you interact. Sometimes, as in the following exercise, you can use them in sequence, and the one may work when the other fails.

Exercise: Using non-judgemental awareness when playing out of tune

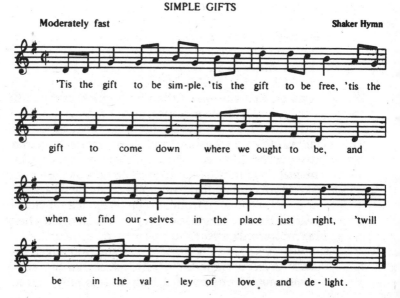

SIMPLE GIFTS

Moderately fast   Shaker Hymn

'Tis the gift to be sim-ple, 'tis the gift to be free, 'tis the gift to come down where we ought to be, and when we find our-selves in the place just right, 'twill be in the val-ley of love and de-light.

Play or sing the Shaker hymn 'Simple Gifts' without criticizing or judging yourself. Just let yourself notice your pitch or intonation.

1. How was your pitch?

2. If you were out of tune, play the piece again, this time paying attention to exactly which notes are out of tune.

3. Now list them. Were these notes sharp or flat? If you didn't notice, play the tune again until you can list which notes you are playing sharp and which ones flat.

4. Now sing or play the piece again, this time focusing your awareness on the notes that were out of tune. Have they changed? For the better? For the worse?

Were you able to correct your problems with pitch and intonation with simple awareness (No.1 of the four ways that awareness can bring about positive change)? By simply noticing which notes were out of tune (No.2)? Once you noticed which notes were sharp or flat (No.3), could you immediately correct them? Or did your awareness when you played the tune again give you subtle feedback that allowed you to make adjustments so that you sang or played in tune (No.4)?

Now let's take a closer look at these four ways, seeing how each in turn can help us deal with the obstacles we all encounter in our playing.

1. Simple awareness may be enough

Tim Gallwey presented his first 'master class' in music at the University of Cincinnati in 1982. No one would have known that he wasn't a trained musician. After the class two piano students approached him with a problem: they were having trouble playing a passage together in a difficult two-piano piece by Franz Liszt.

Tim asked them if they had ever noticed exactly where, on which note, they lost each other. They said they'd never isolated the moment quite that precisely. They only noticed something was wrong after it was all messed up. Tim asked them simply to be aware, and to notice precisely in which bar the difficulty arose during their next practice session.

They came back twenty minutes later and told him that as

soon as they listened for the part where they were playing out of synch, they didn't make any mistakes. They had played the piece correctly for the first time. Awareness cured their problem instantly by giving them a new focus for their attention.

Obviously, when we are in this state of non-judgemental awareness, something different happens: we listen more closely, and this gives our body clues which allow it to adjust at a level below our conscious awareness, without physical or mental interference.

Exercise: Awareness as an Antidote to Trying

Play or sing the passage below. Keep in strict tempo, and *try* to play all the notes accurately the first time:

(*Voice*) ta   ta   ta   *etc.*

Now repeat the same passage. This time don't worry so much about the tempo, simply notice those notes you play inaccurately. List them.

Did you miss more notes the first time or the second? Did you notice any difference between playing while you were *trying* to get the notes right and playing while just remaining aware of which notes were accurate?

Many musicians find there is a big difference between the way they play when they are *trying* and when they are simply being aware. The awareness mode encourages the conscious mind to listen to what's happening, and this increases the amount of feedback we receive, which allows positive changes to occur almost without effort.

When we are *trying*, our awareness is taken away from the music and focused on our 'running commentary'. It turns out that it's very difficult to focus on both at the same time. When Self 1 is absorbing your awareness with its criticisms, instructions and attempts to control your playing, you cannot simultaneously be fully concentrating on and aware of what you are listening to and receiving feedback from your awareness.

2. Accepting the problem the way it is

You can use your awareness to accept a problem, get to know it, and give it permission to be the way it is. This often results in the problem clearing up. Perhaps you've noticed that when you're feeling tense before a performance or an exam, if you tell someone else about your nervousness, the very fact that they accept you, nerves and all, may allow you to feel better.

Shaking the Shakes

I remember a presentation of the Inner Game that Tim made at the Music Educators National Conference in San Antonio, Texas. Tim showed us how he would teach a viola player to shake the shakes – by letting her hands shake as much as they liked, until they settled down of their own accord.

Mary told us her hands were shaking so much that she couldn't hold her bow steady. Tim asked her to put her viola down and show her shaking hands to the audience. Then he asked her, 'Now feel your hands. Which hand is shaking most?' She told him, 'The right hand.' 'Which fingers are shaking most?' he asked. 'The first and second.' 'And of those two fingers, which is shaking more?' 'The first finger.' Tim then asked her to describe the pattern of shaking to the audience. Was it vertical, horizontal or circular? Steady or erratic?

Each time Tim asked her a question and she paid more attention to her hands, the hands would shake a little less. Finally, Mary noticed that her left hand had stopped shaking altogether and that her right was only trembling slightly. Tim asked the audience if it was OK for Mary's right first finger to keep on shaking. They told her it was – but Mary found that the shaking had mysteriously disappeared. It seemed as though her fingers had at last had enough opportunity to shake, and Mary was able to turn her attention back to her performance for the group.

Exercise: Accepting the problem

The next time you feel any of the symptoms of anxiety or nervousness (sweaty hands, shaking knees, dry mouth, fast heartbeat, upset stomach and so on), don't criticize yourself – just see how much you can notice about your present condition. Locate the most severe part of the problem – the part of the stomach that hurts most, or whatever. Then notice whether putting your attention on the problem has caused any changes. Perhaps things have got better? Or worse?

Now see if you can still play the music. When you feel you have familiarized yourself with the extent of the symptom, give it permission to be there, and then choose another focus for your attention. As before, this new focus can be on sight, sound, feeling, or what you know about the piece.

Did this exercise show you that when you become aware of a physical obstacle, even though it may not go away, it has less of an impact on your attention? When you give the problem permission to exist, your attention is free to return to the music. Did you notice that the physical problem tends to disappear as you become more involved in your playing?

Focusing on the middle path

In Chapter 1, we discussed the technique of deliberately increasing and decreasing your tension. We saw how Randy deliberately increased and decreased the level of tension in his forearm and, by noticing the difference in the way his muscles felt, was able to recognize for the first time which muscles were getting in his way.

This technique of pushing some aspect of your playing to an extreme in both directions may remind you of focusing a camera. When you're taking photos, you usually make sure you're in perfect focus by adjusting the ring both ways. The way to get the sharpest focus is to find the point midway between the places where it comes into focus and the point where we can barely notice that it is blurring again.

The same principle is at work when you use the technique of focusing in both directions. This is not limited to dealing with bodily tension, but can also be used to discover a suitable dynamic, tempo or expression for a given piece of music.

Exercise: Focusing on the Middle Path

Play or sing "Simple Gifts" again (page 58).

1. Play it too soft, then too loud, and then the way you feel most comfortable.

2. Play it too fast, then too slow, and then the way you like.

3. Play it with a strong rhythmic emphasis, then romantically, then sadly, then formally, with a carefree spirit, aggressively, gingerly and religiously. There is no one particular 'right way' to play the piece. Experiment with a variety of different styles of expression, and then play it the way you feel best about.

Which way felt best to you when you were focusing the volume toward both ends of the scale? How did you know this was the best? Which tempo worked best for you? How could you tell? Which type of expression did you finally choose? Why? What was it that showed you that this was the best approach?

3. Noticing subtle differences

The example of Randy's 'focusing in both directions' also involved the use of a one-to-ten rating scale. Tim Gallwey showed me another way to use the rating scale, this time without deliberately changing the factor that the scale is measuring. This variation of the exercise is both subtler and more powerful.

Myron complained that he felt some tension in his back while he played the piano. His muscles were tight, and his playing reflected that tightness in a lack of flexibility. I made it clear to Myron that he shouldn't judge himself critically, but simply be aware of his playing and be able to rate his tension on the one-to-ten scale. We agreed to rate his present level of tension as a five on the scale, with a one representing complete lack of tension and a ten representing maximum tension.

Of course, there was likely to be a difference from one reading to the next, even without Myron deliberately altering the tension. After the first five he gave his next reading a four. Then he played a six, and then another four.

Since we were playing a 'rating game' and not a 'fix-it game', Myron became intrigued by the exercise. Without any conscious intention he played a two. This was exciting.

I could see Myron's curiosity and fascination growing by the moment, because he had stumbled on to something that relaxed him – without any conscious effort on his part to relax.

I asked him what was going on. He told me that he was discovering that when he played a two, he could automatically feel where in his body he was holding tension. This gave him a more conscious connection with the muscles in his back – and his back muscles released their grip on his fingers. He could feel his chest, neck and jaw 'letting go' too.

Finally, he told me, 'I've got it,' and played his piece without any stiffness in his back.

When we'd finished the lesson, I asked Myron an interesting question: 'How did you know you'd got it?' Myron answered me with a new note of confidence in his voice: ' For the first time I could feel the precise muscles I needed to relax. I could hear the difference in the sound. The music began to sound the way I wanted it – free and fluid.'

The question 'How do you know that such and such a change has taken place?' helps us to verbalize the feedback we are receiving about subtle changes in our feelings and other senses so that we can take what we have learned and apply it in other circumstances.

4. Finding the problem behind the problem

If you are having a problem with some aspect of your playing such as getting enough air, keeping in tune, or holding a strong rhythm; hitting the right notes; remembering your fingering, the words or the bowing; or letting go of tension in your body, you may find that awareness will lead you to a 'problem behind the problem'.

Awareness can often show us that a problem of this sort is just one symptom of a deeper problem, and when we have dealt with the deeper problem, the symptom goes away as well. Once again, you need to use your sight, hearing, feelings and understanding to show you where the 'problem behind the problem' lies.

A trombonist I met at a workshop, in Minnesota found she was having trouble getting enough air at the ends of her phrases. When I asked her simply to be aware of the sound of the last notes of a phrase, a remarkable change took place.

As she put her attention on those last few notes, she unthinkingly switched from a slide vibrato to a lip vibrato. The phrase sounded much better – and her desperate breathing vanished. She had discovered by her own simple awareness that not having sufficient air wasn't her real problem – her 'problem behind the problem' came from using the wrong kind of vibrato.

A pianist who couldn't figure out a tricky rhythm found his real problem was that he'd lost track of the major beats in the bar. A guitarist couldn't decide what tempo to play a particular piece in, and then realized he'd never heard that kind of music before and needed to do some research. He needed either to talk to someone who was familiar with the genre or listen to some recordings. A singer who thought she needed to take in more air to complete a phrase watched for the exact moment that she gasped for air, and noticed that her body posture was tensing up her stomach muscles so that she was no longer able to expand her lungs from her diaphragm.

In each of these cases, the real problem wasn't what the student thought it was; and when the deeper problem came into awareness, the symptomatic problem cleared up at once.

Awareness has an incredible power to focus our attention, bring us into the present moment with the music we are listening to or playing, enable us to handle distractions and cure a wide variety of problems. But it needs some direction if it is to produce the results we are looking for.

In the next chapter we shall discover how having clear goals can help us to focus our awareness in specific directions. We shall also learn how to identify our goals in the three areas of performance, experience and learning.

5 The power of will

When James McCracken, the famous tenor, was in his late teens, he pasted a small silver star in a corner of his bathroom mirror. He told me that every morning when he went in to shave, that star would remind him of his life's goal – to sing at the Metropolitan Opera.

McCracken's goal gave his life direction and impetus. Because he knew so clearly what he was aiming for, he was able to make the thousand daily choices that would bring him closer to his goal. Within a few years his opportunity came, and he was ready for it.

Goals are the direction-finders for our will, and the major 'will skill' that we need to learn is goal clarity. Tim Gallwey often said to me that the quality of desire determines the quality of our concentration. When we have clear goals and are focused on them, our concentration can be sustained.

Martial arts such as karate and aikido have demonstrated the tremendous physical reserves that are available to a disciplined and strong will focused on clear goals. When we are clear about our musical goals, we find that similar reserves of strength and energy become available to us. On the other hand, when we are uncertain about our goals, it is hard to bring our will to bear on them and easy for our concentration to wander.

Degrees of Distraction

Let's take a look at some of the ways in which our attention and concentration can be diverted when we are concerned with issues apart from the music itself.

We have all probably experienced times when there was little or no internal conversation or interference to distract us. At these times we were able to focus on the music and put all our energy into it.

100% concentration ─────────────────→ 100% music

Equally, we all know that when our attention is divided between the music and other factors, such as winning an audition, appearing attractive or impressing our colleagues, we provide Self 1 with some splendid opportunities to interfere with our performance.

The point to notice here is that even if you're only paying attention to one other factor, your capacity to focus on the music may already have been cut in half.

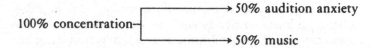

100% concentration─┐ → 50% audition anxiety
                   └ → 50% music

And when our attention is shifting back and forth between five or more different concerns, hopes, worries and interests, our concentration on the music may be even less.

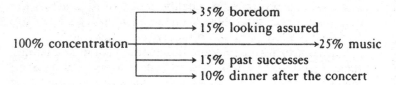

100% concentration─┬→ 35% boredom
                   ├→ 15% looking assured
                   ├────────────→ 25% music
                   ├→ 15% past successes
                   └→ 10% dinner after the concert

We all know how dangerous distractions can be, of course, and yet how often do we think about these things and let our choice (to focus on the music and turn aside from distraction) influence our actual practice?

Why do we choose music?

'People compose for many reasons,' the composer Robert Schumann once remarked: 'to become immortal; because the piano happens to be open; because they want to become a millionaire; because of the praise of friends; because they have looked into a pair of beautiful eyes; or for no reason whatsoever.'

Why do you love music? When was the last time you even asked yourself the question? What part does music play in your life? What is your overall musical goal? Do you intend to make music your profession? To play for your own delight, or that of your friends? Or is it that you glimpsed 'a pair of beautiful eyes'?

Exercise: Reasons for choosing music

Ask yourself how listening to or playing music makes you feel. Music can be a way for us to experience love, excitement, joy, sadness and even spiritual fulfilment. List the ways in which it affects you.

Do you enjoy sharing your music with others? If so, how?

What opportunities does your music give you that you don't otherwise experience?

When I have asked my music students these questions, some of them have found they didn't want to answer them too hastily. I was reaching into a very personal part of their being, and they wanted to answer me as truthfully as they could.

After some reflection almost all of them began by saying that they love music and they enjoy playing it. Many of them went on to say that music is a way for them to learn more, or to perform publicly, and some of them told me it gave them a chance to play out their fantasies. Lastly, many of them quietly admitted that one of life's greatest pleasures came when they were able to share their joy in music with others.

In order to meet your long-term goals, you will also want to narrow in on specific goals every time you practise. In Chapter 3, we examined the P.E.L. triangle and saw that there are three types of goals available to players of the Inner Game: performance (achievement), experience and learning.

When we find an appropriate balance of these three areas, we can achieve and sustain a relaxed concentration and express our potential to the fullest. Let's look at each area in turn and examine some examples of performance, experience and learning goals.

Performance Goals in Music

'Music is the space between the notes,' Claude Debussy once remarked. The notations on the printed page are like a blueprint – they let you know what you are supposed to play, and can contribute to your understanding of how to phrase it. But they can only take you so far. Every conductor will have his own interpretation of a given piece of music, and the all-important differences in style and approach between Herbert von Karajan and Neville Marriner come from within the conductors themselves.

Performance goal 1: using visual cues

The printed page, if you like, represents only a small percentage of the music (perhaps only 10 per cent), and the remainder comes from your interpretation and personal expression of the text. A reading that lacks this personal element will sound flat and mechanical; one that includes it will sound alive.

The purpose of the score is to give you the bare bones – the skeleton or structure of the piece – so that you can then go beyond it into your own musicality and personal interpretation.

Few people make full use of this skeletal structure. We seldom observe every mark on the printed page – every note, dynamic marking, accent and rhythm. And yet a detailed reading of the text and familiarity with it is the first step in allowing your musicianship to come through.

Jonas Starker, cello professor at Indiana University, understood this need for a close study of the text. He would often ask his students to memorize all the visual markings in a Bach cello suite before they began to actually play it. Then he would test their recall by asking them to write out all the notes, fingerings, bowings, phrasings, dynamics and rhythms. When they had become thoroughly familiar with the material in this way, he was confident they could turn their attention to playing the music 'between the notes'.

I am not suggesting that you should be able to write out all the notes and markings of every piece you play. But the performance goal of familiarizing yourself with the score in detail before you start playing can free you from the printed page so you can give more of your attention to matters of interpretation and expression.

Exercise: Freeing the eye from watching the notes

1. Play or sing Bach's Minuet in G, looking at every note as you play it.

2. Play it again, until you feel familiar with the piece and its markings. Now repeat the melody, this time letting your eyes run ahead to the next bar when you have reminded yourself of the notes and markings in the present one.

3. Now play the melody without music, using your inner sense of the music to guide you.

4. Play it again without music, this time using your visual imagination to sense what your fingers and body look like while you're playing.

5. Now imagine that you are Bach himself, playing your minuet in a candlelit ballroom filled with noblemen in wigs and velvet coats and their ladies in ruffled gowns. Play the piece one last time, perhaps with your eyes closed, and watch the dancers . . .

How has your playing changed in the course of the exercise? How was your performance when you were studying the music note for note? When you were just glancing briefly at the music? When you left the musical cues behind and played without music?

Most musicians find that the further they remove themselves from the image of the printed score, the more they can express that part of the music that comes from inside them.

This exercise used the printed score as a series of musical cues and explored the possibility of becoming familiar with them, internalizing them, and then being able to leave them behind. It also made use of other kinds of performance goals that make use of sight and vision – 'seeing' yourself performing and 'imagining' a scene that relates to the music.

Performance goal 2: using physical cues

Your body can also provide you with performance clues, and you may find it useful to set yourself 'kin-aesthetic' or body goals.

When I worked with dancers, I discovered that although choreographers do have a written notation for the various moves they want the dancers to perform, the dancers themselves seldom work from it. The instructor or choreographer demonstrates a series of movements while the dancers watch. Then the dancers form a mental image of what they have seen and imagine their own bodies recreating the movements. Finally, when they have both seen the moves and 'felt through them' in their bodies, they are able to execute the moves on the dance floor.

Feeling the moves 'in your body' allows you to rehearse them before you 'go through the motions'. Recent findings suggest that this style of 'kinaesthetic' rehearsal actually programmes and makes use of those parts of the nervous system that will be involved in physical execution.

Using your body's kinaesthetic memory in this way prepares the body for accurate performance.

Exercise: Kinaesthetic preparation

For this exercise you can use the Bach Minuet in G again or some other piece of your own choice.

1. Before you start playing or singing the first phrase, imagine your body playing the piece. Allow your body to make just enough miniature muscle movements to ensure

that your 'image' is connecting with your body's own kinaesthetic way of knowing.

2. When you feel comfortable with this kinaesthetic
rehearsal of the piece, play or sing the piece out loud.

3. When you come across a difficult leap, change of register or fast passage – or even when you find you need to learn
some of the notes – practise away from the instrument, using
your kinaesthetic sense, until you feel completely confident
and comfortable.

4. Go back to your instrument, or begin singing out loud
again, and notice how your body can now more easily follow
the patterns that you have stored in your kinaesthetic
memory.

The philosopher Ludwig Wittgenstein was an accomplished pianist and used to practise entire piano concertos
without a keyboard to pass the time on long train journeys.
When he hit a wrong note – without a keyboard – he would
go back and correct it.

Many musicians spend a great deal of their time practising
'away from their instruments' and find it to be musically
effective, as well as offering them a chance to work on their
music when they wouldn't otherwise be able to.

The body's kinaesthetic sense is an important part of musicianship. Dancing, singing, foot tapping and 'conducting
along with the record' are other ways to engage the body
with the music.

The strutting and dancing on stage that so many rock
musicians use in concert is another example of this kinaesthetic approach (quite apart from the impact it has on the
audience). When rock stars go into the studio to cut a record,
they often have a hard time getting their performance right
because the space limitations of the studio prevent them from
'dancing the music' in a way that is essential to their total
delivery.

Performance goal 3: the authentic sound

If we are to communicate a piece of music effectively
in the spirit in which it was intended, we need to know and
respect the composer's goal. The performance goal in music

is usually to play the music accurately and in the proper style
– making jazz swing, and giving Mozart a certain elegance.

For instance, to be able to play everything from Baroque
and Classical to Romantic and new music, you need to
become familiar with their stylistic differences. Much of this
shading can be learned by listening to recordings. You can
also explore authentic performance practices in discussion
with other players and your teachers.

As a jazz player you might try imitating one of your favourite performers. This will help you to build up your subconscious knowledge of which style, tempo or articulation
sounds best. Many great jazz artists openly admit to having
memorized some of the best solos of their favourite models
note for note. George Gershwin said he made his early songs
sound as much like Jerome Kern's as he possibly could.

Studio musicians take pride in their ability to play any
arrangement at sight in its appropriate style. Recording time
is very expensive, and producers expect the musicians to
know and deliver the subtle differences between jazz,
country music, disco, rock, Broadway and 'middle-of-the-
road'. These musicians are very clear about their performance
goals. They are not there to be 'artists', but skilled craftsmen
who can deliver whatever stylistic interpretation the arrangement calls for.

Performance goal 4: the music in your head

Many of us have heard our teachers say 'If you can't
hear it in your head, you can't play it.' The Suzuki method
teaches children to play music without reading it, and uses
recordings to give them an idea of the way the music should
sound.

When we're having a problem playing a passage in tune,
it's often because we aren't 'hearing' the music. Most people
can hear a melodic range in their heads that is much greater
than their voice can sing – a range which generally includes
all the notes that are possible on any instrument. In other
words, when you are looking at a musical score or thinking

about a piece of music, your imagination can 'hear' all the notes, including the chords.

When you can hold the sound and pitch of the music clearly in your head in this way, performing it accurately becomes easier. Your body has a sense of its goal. Effectively, you are playing a duet between the music in your head and the music you are performing. Any notes you play that don't correspond to your imagined sense of the music stand out, and your nervous system is able to make instant, unconscious adjustments.

If you don't already have this kind of detailed sense of the music in your head, making corrective adjustments becomes a longer and more complex task. First, you have to notice your errors. Then you need to decide what adjustment is needed. And by the time you get around to making the adjustment, the note has come and gone already.

You may have seen the celebrated pianist André Watts appear to sing along as he played, or heard Keith Jarrett groan in sympathy with the music. They are 'hearing' the music inside as they play. If your performance goal is to 'hear' the music as you are playing it, you will be able to shape your performance to what you 'hear' inside you. You will be able to play with greater fluidity and accuracy.

Exercise: Hearing the music you play

Play or sing this music without first studying the whole piece or 'running it through' in your head. Notice the way you phrase the piece rhythmically – until you recognize the melody. Then you can stop.

You probably recognized the melody as 'Camptown Races' by Stephen Foster. Now read the melodic line through in your mind, remind yourself of the way the tune sounds, and play it again, this time 'hearing' the sound inside you as you play.

Now play a selection of your choice, a piece that you know well and can 'hear' in your head, even if you can only read it at a very slow tempo and can only complete one or two bars at a time.

Did you notice any difference when you played while 'hearing' the piece inside you? Did your playing become more flexible, impassioned and alive?

Performance goal 5: the meaning of the music

Some musical pieces, such as Mussorgsky's *Pictures at an Exhibition*, are 'programme' pieces, written to express a specific atmosphere or story in sound. Most orchestral and instrumental music, however, is not.

We have already discussed the possibility of exploring the authentic style of a piece. Another performance goal that will help you convey the composer's intended effect to your audience is to express the meaning and emotions of the music. To give your performance a new sense of conviction and colour, you can create your own 'programme' for a piece of music.

Performance goal 6: the drama in the music

Charles was performing a moody and evocative Spanish guitar piece by Manuel de Falla. I noticed that Charles' performance, although accurate in terms of notes and dynamics, somehow wasn't expressing the full emotional impact of the piece.

I asked Charles to imagine a story that could accompany the various shifts of mood and emotion in the piece. As he played the repetitive, mysterious opening measures, he said the music reminded him of a misty forest at daybreak. Then he 'saw' a fugitive running from his pursuers. He came to some sharp, high chords, and commented that they suggested the frightened man making sudden changes of direction in an attempt to throw off his pursuers. Then the piece returned to the opening mood with some lower-pitched chords. Charles felt the fugitive was looking back through the branches of the forest to see whether his pursuers were still following. Suddenly, the captors surround the fugitive, as the music shifts to a series of aggressive leaps and outbursts of staccato rhythm, accompanied by loud percussive sounds on the body of the guitar. Finally, the fugitive escapes into the forest, and the music returns to the calm mood of the opening measures.

When I asked Charles to 'visualize' this story (without this time telling it out loud) as he performed the piece, his final performance was much more exciting and convincing.

Exercise: Putting meaning into your music

Choose a piece of music with a title that indicates excitement or energy – *Presto, Scherzo, Tarantella, Mazurka, Hunter's Song, Burlesque, Polonaise.*

1. Identify the themes or motifs in the music that give the piece the energy in the title.

2. Assign different characters to go with these motifs and themes.

3. Imagine a situation or create a story that involves these characters and which fits the overall shape of the piece.

4. Emphasize these 'character' motifs with appropriate dynamics, accents or articulations.

5. Don't worry about how accurately you play all the notes. Play the piece, allowing your story and characters to give their strength to your interpretation.

You will probably find that when you put your emphasis on expressing the drama of the music, you will be more effective in communicating its meaning.

Experience Goals in Music

Paying attention to the way we feel when we are practising or performing is as important as having clear performance goals.

Deborah Armstrong was the first American to win a gold medal at the 1984 Winter Olympic Games. After winning an upset victory over the world's top-ranking giant slalom skiers, she told an interviewer: 'I didn't do anything special . . . I didn't think about my skiing, I just thought about having fun. I turned to my teammates in the chute just before the run and said "I'm gonna have a good time." ' She agreed that her mental attitude was probably the major cause of her victory.

Just a few days after Deborah Armstrong's Olympic triumph, I was performing with the Cincinnati Symphony at Carnegie Hall. I was playing several bass solos in two difficult contemporary pieces, and I was worried about the response I'd get from the audience – and the legendary New York critics.

Deborah Armstrong's remarks gave me the inspiration I needed. I decided to set an experience goal for my performance. I, too, would make a point of 'having fun'. Although it took some courage for me to let go of my fear and stop worrying that I would miss notes, I concentrated on my experience goal – to enjoy playing. It worked. I was caught up in the experience of making music, and my performance was well received.

I am often impressed with the spontaneity, confidence and enthusiasm of amateur musicians, as well as by the excellent music they often make. Yet if you ask amateur musicians to play a Beethoven sonata in public or for pay, they'll often decline the invitation. 'I just want to enjoy my music,' they explain. 'Playing in public would probably make me nervous, and it wouldn't be any fun.'

'Amateur' has come to mean 'non-professional' or 'unpaid'. But the word is derived from the French *aimer* ('to love') and literally means someone who 'loves' what they do. The true amateur, then, is someone whose attitude to music never loses sight of their experience goal.

Two kinds of experience goal

We need to distinguish between two types of experience goal. The first kind has to do with the way you feel about *yourself* when you're playing or practising music: it may include such things as feeling tense or calm, struggling with the music or mastering it, feeling overwhelmed by Self 1 worries, or delighted by Self 2's musicianship. The second kind has to do with your experience of the *music* – of the qualities and emotions the piece itself conveys: the grandeur of the Saint-Saëns *Organ* Symphony, or the melancholy behind the blues.

The ultimate goal of our playing or listening is to merge into the music. If you feel tense and worried about your fingering when you're playing a delicate passage from a Bach adagio, you're less likely to be able to let the delicacy of the music speak through you. It's important to move toward the point where you're comfortable with your experience of *yourself* in the act of playing, so that your *musical* experience can come through.

Sometimes you may feel tense about a piece before it's actually time for you to begin playing. Sometimes before I'm to play a short solo in the orchestra, I begin to worry about the way I'll perform. At times like these I set myself an experience goal from the first category – feeling comfortable and not worrying about my performance before I begin to play. Then I give myself some other focus of awareness: I focus on my breathing, perhaps, or on a section of the orchestra that's already playing. When the time comes for me to play, I switch to a goal from the second group – 'becoming' the music I'm playing.

What kinds of experience goals do you have when you are practising by yourself? When you are rehearsing with a group? Or when you are playing in a concert or recital?

Do your performance goals crowd out your experience goals to the point where you lose track of them completely? If music was once a real joy but has become something of a grind over the course of time, reinstating your original experience goals may be the way to restore your love.

In setting your experience goals you may want to start with

goals that have to do with your experience of Self 1 interference, and move on to goals that deal with your actual experience of music when the interference is dealt with. It's hard to have a good experience of the music until both your mental interference patterns and any major technical problems have been dealt with.

I asked Regina to play a modern piece for flute, and she played it excellently. I had no comments to make about her technique, so I asked her what aspect of the piece she'd like to work on. She told me she was happy with her technical command of the piece, but that she didn't feel she was catching the mood of the piece as she played it. Playing in the classroom under bright lights was not helping any. Regina told me she felt detached and uninvolved.

I asked Regina what she sensed the piece was about, and she said its overall mood seemed to express a stark or 'barren' quality. It was winter, so I suggested she go outside to look at a tree stripped bare of its leaves. When she came back into the room, I asked her to close her eyes and visualize the tree as a symbol of the 'barren' quality of the music.

When she opened her eyes, Regina wasn't thinking about the harsh lighting and the people around her: she was still feeling the starkness and barren quality of the tree she'd visualized. She played the piece with magnificent feeling, as if she were in another world.

If only I'd known this way back when

When I think about the way I approached learning music before I realized how central the goal of real expression was, I feel ashamed and embarrassed.

There's a solo piece for the bass by Reinhold Glière that I still play from time to time. It's called *Tarantella*. A tarantella is a Neapolitan dance in 6/8 time, and this particular tarantella is written to be performed as fast as you can possibly play.

When I first learned this piece, I studied it note by note. My progress (and my playing) was slow at first. I never exactly sat down and memorized the piece, but by the time I was ready to play it in public, I no longer needed to watch every note on the page. As I played it, it sounded very much the way I thought about it – like a pile of fast notes tumbling one on top of another.

These days I approach the piece differently. I no longer think about all those black dots on the page. I've learned there's a wide-spread legend that the tarantella is named after a spider, the tarantula, whose poisonous bite was a serious problem in southern Italy in the Middle Ages. Apparently, the people of those times believed that this furious dance would cure the spider's bite – hence the name.

The dance has taken on a new meaning for me. Instead of concentrating on all those fast shifts, flurries of notes, bowings and fingerings, I allow myself to feel the panic and energy of a poisoned villager dancing as though life itself depended on it.

Learning goals in music

The very word 'learning' brings up classroom memories of boredom, frustration and tedious repetition for many of us. Yet when we don't challenge ourselves, stretching to make new discoveries, we are likely to experience stagnation and mediocrity.

If you recall your most outstanding performances, you may notice that they often occurred during those sessions when a long period of learning suddenly 'clicked'. Entering a learning spiral can deliver immense satisfaction. We reach new heights by building on what we already know. The mastery of new information or technique contributes to our confidence, which can further inspire us to learn and accomplish even more.

Noticing our growth as it occurs helps to provide us with the encouragement and discipline to continue learning. When we are unaware of our growth, it can be hard for us to muster the motivation to keep on working. But when we can see the value of learning, and have discovered some simple, effective processes for creating the sound we want, we will find that our continued effort is continually rewarding.

We need to start by getting our performance goals clear,

since our learning goals will often be determined by them. Then we can formulate our learning goals and allow our brain and body to work at them – one or two at a time.

Sometimes we go over the same piece again and again. We hope we will eventually play the notes accurately and that the dynamics, style, pitch, bowings, fingerings and articulations will finally fall into place. I have found that this approach doesn't work too well, because we learn most effectively when we focus on just one problem at a time.

The body, like a computer, remembers its instructions when it has been properly programmed. But like even the most sophisticated computer, it needs to be programmed 'a bit at a time'.

I have chosen another familiar melody for this exercise so that our performance goal (knowing how it should sound) will be simple. As usual, you should feel free to substitute another piece of your own choosing for this one by Stephen Foster.

Exercise: Learning the melody

1. Play or sing Foster's 'Beautiful Dreamer'.

2. List your learning goals. In order to put what you need to learn into words, you may want to ask yourself some leading questions, and make a list of your answers:

●   Was this the best I've ever played this piece? If not, where did my playing fall down this time?

●   What did I definitely like about the way I played? What would I change to make it better?

●   If I were playing (or singing) this piece six months from now, what improvements woud I expect to find in my playing?

A typical list of learning goals might look like this:

    a. Intonation in bar 3.
    b. Rhythmic problems with 7, 8 and 9.
    c. Missed notes in 7 and 8.
    d. Rough phrasing.
    e. Tempo too slow.
    f. Fingerings don't work in bar 8.

3. What are your three biggest problems, in order of importance? List them. For example:

    a. Intonation
    b. Fingering
    c. Phrasing.

4. Find the precise place where the problem arises. Use your awareness skills to locate 'What' is going wrong, 'Where', 'When', and 'How Much'.

Suppose your learning goal had to do with intonation, the first priority on the previous list. You might locate your problem like this:

WHAT:	Intonation.
WHERE:	In bars 7 and 8.
WHEN:	The B in 7 and the F in 8.
HOW MUCH:	B is very sharp; F is a little flat.

If you have trouble coming up with answers to these four questions, you need to play the piece again, with even more simple awareness of what is happening. Don't forget that some of your answers may involve such things as tension in your muscles, or breathing patterns. Awareness can locate the source of your problem wherever it is. But you need to give your awareness the freedom to go about it.

5. Simply notice the problem as it is. Perhaps your problem will clear itself up as soon as your awareness focuses on the exact point where something is going wrong. Sometimes the solution will be obvious to you and you will be able to fix it yourself. And sometimes you will have to use some of the

further awareness techniques discussed in Chapter 4, such as looking for the 'problem behind the problem' (page 64).

6. Once your first-priority problem is solved, move on down your list to the next, and repeat this process, starting with 'What', 'Where', 'When' and 'How Much'.

This process can help you achieve all your learning goals, at any level from beginning to advanced playing, whatever your instrument. Simply set yourself clear learning goals and address them one at a time. When awareness provides you with the solutions to your problems, you can trust that the solutions will continue to work as long as you keep your concentration focused on the music and in the present.

Juggling your goals

Earlier in this chapter we saw that when your attention was split between the music and the various worries and concerns of Self 1, the result wasn't too favourable. Yet we have spent this chapter exploring a number of different kinds of goal – performance, experience and learning goals; goals using sight, imagination and body feedback; and goals focused on your feeling of the music.

Perhaps you have wondered if all these goals won't split your attention and diminish your concentration in much the same way as the Self 1 concerns did – and with equally unfavourable results. You'll probably find they don't, for the simple reason that performance, experience and learning goals dovetail with each other.

What's more, you don't have to focus your attention on your goals all the time. When you're going to drive to a concert, you certainly set yourself the goal of driving there, and switch on the ignition. But then you let go of your goal, and turn your attention to traffic conditions and the road ahead of you.

If you set yourself goals in terms of your music and then allow yourself to forget about them and return your focus to sight, sound, feeling and so on, you'll find your goals are working for you at a subconscious level.

You have probably noticed, too, that technical problems, and any interference you may have, tend to get in the way of real concentration on your musical feelings, but that it is only when your attention is finally on your feelings that the music really comes alive.

Your goals reflect the stage you have reached in relation to each individual piece. As you move from focusing on the more technical aspects to attending to the feeling, you may find you need to risk missing more notes or losing some of your sense of being in control. Don't worry. It's just fine to risk missing some notes.

If you do miss some notes, don't blame yourself. You can certainly return to your technical goals later. Nobody gets to Carnegie Hall or the Met without practising. But you'll often be surprised by how accurately you play when you relax and let the feelings come through you.

There's very little to be said for learning a piece note by note, reading the rhythmic markings, practising the fingerings and following all your instructor's suggestions, if you haven't any idea how the music will eventually sound and feel. If you learn a piece mechanically, you may have to 'unlearn' it before you can play it with expression and feeling.

I'd like to make one other point. Learning goals are by no means limited to the learning of techniques that improve your performance, although that kind of learning is obviously important. You can also give yourself learning goals as you are going about the business of playing music that will help you in your life outside the practice chamber or the concert hall. You can have a learning goal to improve your concentration, or to handle fear of failure – and these lessons will provide you with skills that are invaluable in every part of your life.

Exercise: Moving through the different goals

Let's take a look at 'Old Man River'.

J. Kern

1. First, let yourself remember this beautiful old song. Perhaps you recall Paul Robeson singing it. Hear the song in your head.

2. Now look at the music again and begin to play a few notes or measures at a time.

3. When you're ready, repeat the process, this time without looking at the music.

4. Now play it 'for the sound'. Notice the difference in the way you play.

5. Now play for the feeling of the music. Imagine that 'old man' rolling along. Even if you still have to look at the notes, keep your attention on the feelings. Let them pour through you.

You probably discovered you learned the piece much faster this way. The fact that you were working from your memory of the piece probably helped you get over any worries you might have had about forgetting the notes. And the feeling – isn't that what playing 'Old Man River' is all about?

Goal setting for the future

At the International Summer Bass School, Paul Ellison, principal bass player of the Houston Symphony, suggested keeping a goal journal. He first learned the system at a workshop for personal time management and saw that it had obvious applications for music students and teachers.

The goal journal proved to be such a useful tool for our students at the Summer Bass School that I tried it with my Cincinnati Conservatory students in the autumn. I asked them to keep a journal that listed daily goals, as well as their plans for the next five or ten years. Writing in the journal every day kept them constantly reminded of their long- and short-term goals, in much the same way that James McCracken's star kept him focused on his goal of singing at the Met. And when their daily activities didn't support their long-term goals, they began to look for ways to fine-tune one or the other.

I found that this process gave the students a new sense of responsibility for their own futures. They came to class with lists of the problems they were currently working on. They knew what their priorities were, and the lessons became better organized and more fulfilling for all of us.

The journals also provided the students with an invaluable record of the problems addressed and the discoveries they'd made during lessons. Over a period of time they became so good at focusing in on their learning goals that they often eliminated them before they came to class – and sometimes even before they'd written them down.

They learned to strike a balance between their goals in the different areas of performance, experience and learning. And when they were clear on their goals, they'd allow them to settle into the subconscious, and begin to practise.

After working with her journal for several months, bass player Marie Wallace wrote: 'It was pretty scary at first to see my goals written down in black and white – but it made them *real*. Practising isn't the effort it used to be. I see it now as a way to achieve my goals, not as something I have to do and somewhat resent. And I now evaluate things by seeing how much they contribute to the long-range results I'm looking for. For me, that's a 180-degree turn-around . . '

To create your own goal journal all you need is a loose-leaf book. Let's take a look at some sample entries. Obviously, your longer-range goals won't need as much space as your daily goals, but it's probably helpful to keep the longer-range goals at the beginning so that you're reminded of them every time you open your journal.

1. Long-range goals – five to ten years

These are probably your ultimate career or life goals. Typical entries in this section might include: getting a position in a major symphony, teaching at a major university, having a career as a soloist or chamber musician, or singing with Woody Herman's band.

2. Medium-range goals – one to five years

Typical entries: prepare for senior recital, complete technical studies for my instrument, work on techniques for overcoming fear and doubt, obtain engagements in regional clubs and theatres, obtain employment in a semi-professional organization, learn a repertoire for auditioning and interviewing.

3. Short-range goals – two to fifteen weeks

Typical entries: work out fingering, bowing and phrasing and learn spiccato technique for the Mozart sonata; memorize and polish for recital at the retirement home; *OR* learn three 45-minute vocal sets for the Hyatt Hotel lounge audition.

4. This Week's Goals

The entries here usually refer to specific movements in the pieces you are working on.

Typical entries: learn first movement and half of second movement of Mozart sonata, study recording of last movement; *OR* memorize words to three songs, go to hear jazz singer at the Westin lounge.

5. Today's Goals

This will be the longest and most detailed list: it's the one you work from yourself when you're practising, and one that your teacher can work from when you're having a lesson.

Typical entries: first movement of Mozart sonata, work out bowings in bars 4, 5 and 8; decide phrasing in the bar before repeat; intonation in lines 3 and 4; clarify articulation in semiquavers – crisper staccato in bars 23 and 24; *OR Funny Girl*, work out pitch on high notes, expression in the text, free up the rhythm, smooth out transition to high register at climax of the song.

6. Next Week's Goals

These include some items that you've selected from your two-to-fifteen-week goals.

Typical entries: continue with the last movement of the Mozart, work up to performance tempo; practise Kaiser Études numbers 23 and 24; *OR* work on second medley of vocal numbers from Broadway hits.

As the different time periods go by and your various goals are met, make sure you keep your journal up to date. Add new pages to each section when they're needed. By all means, put a line through the goals you've achieved – but don't throw out your old lists.

After they'd been using a goal journal for eighteen months, I found my students were improving dramatically. They were more confident about their ability to solve problems than ever before and found that looking back over their journal notes gave them a sense of accomplishment.

Keeping clear about your goals allows your will to go to work for you.

Reading a new book can be like reading a score for the first time. You want to get beyond the musical notes and the words of the written text to the music and meaning that are hidden in them.

There's something behind what I'm telling you in this book: there's a feeling I'm trying to express, and another feeling that I'm trying to draw out of you by way of response. It's the sense that your own real musicianship needs to come through, past the chatter of Self 1 and any problems with technique, and express itself. The drama, the energy and stillness in the music need to come through.

If, from the moment you start to learn a piece, you can keep in mind what it is that you are playing, how it will sound, and what feeling or meaning you want to express, these sounds will emerge in the quality of your performance. You need to invest your hours of discipline with a clear knowledge of your ultimate destination – to re-create the very essence of the music.

That's the meaning behind my writing this book – the ninety per cent of the 'music' that's between my notes. Your real goal is to transmit an experience of music. Behind and beyond the arpeggios and pizzicatos, the plectrums and the reeds, the rosin, hammers and valves: incredible, unbelievable music.

6 The power of trust

When Pearl Bailey was still an unknown singer, she went to visit her brother Willie, who was already a successful vaudeville dancer in New York. She had had some success singing in the small coal-town clubs of western Pennsylvania and now was ready to try for the big time.

There were two or three major theatres in Harlem then, and Pearl decided to enter one of the Harlem Opera House's Amateur Night competitions. Amateur Nights were showcases for the many near-professional musicians in New York, and the competition was stiff. Pearl dressed herself to perfection, went down to the Opera House – and arrived too late to sign up.

Many others might have been disappointed and would have given up at that point. But Pearl Bailey trusted. She trusted her talent and her commitment. She trusted that all the work she'd put in, the discipline, the late nights, the two-bit clubs really added up to something. She trusted she had what it took. She trusted in herself.

Pearl Bailey didn't give up at the first closed door she came to. She went on from the Harlem Opera House to the Apollo, another excellent theatre which was also holding its Amateur Night that night – and won, with her rendition of Duke Ellington's 'Solitude'.

Long after she became famous, Pearl Bailey would tell the story, adding how glad she finally was that she came too late to compete at the Opera House that night. 'I doubt if I would have made it there,' she said, 'for that night a young girl walked on that stage, opened her mouth, and the audience that had started to snicker ended up cheering . . . Her name was Ella Fitzgerald. She won, and that voice will go down in history.'

Trust: the third Inner Game skill

This chapter is about trust: not blind trust, but the trust that comes after hard work, and the trust that comes from knowing there is music inside you.

We have seen that our awareness and will skills are powerful tools that can help us solve problems and give intensity and direction to our music. In order to achieve our ultimate goal and enter the state of relaxed concentration where we are one with the music, there is one more skill we need. We need to *trust* ourselves.

The barriers to trust

Trust isn't the kind of thing you exactly learn – you either trust or you don't. And when you feel you can't trust, you can't let go. So why is it sometimes so difficult to trust? I've found that there are often obstacles between us and our capacity to trust, and in order to overcome them, we first need to know what they are and how they work.

Would you be willing to give your next recital before a distinguished audience of peers, teachers and music critics with a notable spaghetti stain on your shirtfront? Or using a clarinet you have never played before? Or performing a piece you weren't confident was within your capacity?

Probably you wouldn't – and rightly so.

The reason is simple: you'd have good reason to doubt that things would work out well. You might spend hours, perhaps in the middle of your insomnia, fearing they would turn out disastrously. You wouldn't feel comfortable, in control – or trusting.

You wouldn't give your next recital with a large stain on your shirt because you'd feel embarrassed – your self-image would be at risk. You wouldn't use an instrument you'd never played before because you wouldn't feel in control of the situation. And you wouldn't play a piece you didn't feel confident of because the anxiety might ruin your performance even if nothing else did.

These three examples indicate three major obstacles to trust: worries about your self-image, the feeling that things are out of your control, and doubts and fears about your own ability.

Exercise: Discovering the barriers to trust

In real-life situations these doubts and worries tend to get tangled up in one another. The person who's embarrassed by the spaghetti stain might say they were worried because it made them feel out of control of the social situation, or that their anxiety about how they looked was making them so tense that they weren't sure their sensitive musicianship would be able to come through.

In general, however, the obstacles to our trusting tend to cluster in one of three areas. Which barriers most often come between you and your ability to trust?

1. Do you tend to have problems with your self-image?

   a. Are you concerned about the respect your peers feel for you?

   b. Are you concerned about what the audience will think of your playing?

   c. Are you worried you will be a failure?

2. Do you tend to doubt your control of the situation?

   a. Do you feel stuck with a 'flat' or 'rigid' interpretation?

   b. Are you unable to loosen up and play creatively?

   c. Are you uncomfortable taking risks in your performance?

3. Do you tend to doubt your abilities?

   a. Are you worried you just 'don't have it' musically?

   b. Do you suffer from performance anxiety?

   c. Are you doubtful of your capacity to perform under pressure?

If you want to phrase your own problem more specifically, feel free to do so. But also notice that your obstacles basically boil down to one sort of fear or another – usually in one of these three categories.

Worrying about what others will think of you

The double bass is not known as a solo instrument. However, there's a short bass solo at the beginning of Gustav Mahler's First Symphony which is famous for its difficulty.

The movement begins with the kettledrums in the distance beating the solemn cadence of a funeral procession. As the music comes closer, the bass plays a very exposed solo in a minor key. Being a little afraid about this Mahler First bass solo is understandable. Like the pinch hitter getting his big chance only after all the bases are loaded, the solo bass player may be so nervous he or she can hardly hold the bow.

When the Mahler First was on the symphony programme recently, my fellow orchestra members all assumed I would dispatch the solo with nerves of steel – using all my Inner Game techniques. I felt my reputation was on the line.

I used all my awareness techniques (feel the string vibration, look at the bow, listen to the sound of the phrase, feel the pulse in my body, understand the essence of the music), had all of my musical goals in order, and was doing everything I knew to make the solo sound great.

When I played the solo in rehearsal, it sounded terrible. I panicked and called Tim for help. He was out of town, but his former assistant, Erika Andersen, gave me an Inner Game lesson over the phone. After listening while I explained my whole situation, she pointed out that I was losing my focus on the music by worrying about my reputation and that of the Inner Game. She told me she suspected my performance wasn't working because I'd put all my attention on my *awareness* and *will* techniques and forgotten to *trust* myself. And she suggested that I had problems with my self-image, compounded by the fear that my fellow musicians' whole impression of the Inner Game was on the line.

Music is a performing art

The secret of getting past your worries about how you'll appear to others is to give yourself the character and emotions of the music. You become the music, not yourself.

When I see actress Meryl Streep performing a role like that of Karen Silkwood or Sophie (in *Sophie's Choice*), I get very little feeling for what Meryl Streep herself is like as a person. But I do get a powerful feeling for the character she is portraying. She has the wonderful ability to submerge herself in the role she is playing.

Like actors and actresses, musicians are performing artists. Their job isn't to express their own personalities, but to let the 'character' of the music speak through them. They have a responsibility to express the qualities of the music rather than to exhibit their own personality.

If Rachmaninoff has written a romantic, delicate and feminine piece, it needs to be played that way. A performer who brought too much rugged strength to the piece would be doing no service to Rachmaninoff, the audience, or himself.

When we accept our role as interpreters of the composer's music, we cease to be so worried about how we appear to others. It becomes easier for us to let go of our inhibitions and the kind of self-consciousness that blocks us from enjoying the music.

Leonard Bernstein once said: 'The only way I have of knowing I've done a really remarkable performance is when I lose my ego completely and become the composer. I have the feeling that I'm creating the piece, writing the piece on stage, just click, click, click, making it up as I go, along with those hundred people who are also making it up with me.'

Kató Havas, the great violin teacher and author of *Stage Fright*, says that her goal in music is to 'eliminate the self'. 'The player needs to be able to forget about himself,' she writes. 'This is when real communication begins. For with the elimination of the self, he is able to reach the very core of the music, and is free to transmit it.'

The feeling of being out of control

It's not hard to trust yourself to sing when you're in the privacy of your shower. It's something you know you can do – you don't feel you need to 'try' to do it, so you're not worried about things getting out of control. You can start and stop when you like, you don't have to be concerned about how you sound, you can let go of your inhibitions – and it's delightful. But it's hard to maintain the same trust when you're faced with a harder or more important task. It feels very different to take a master class in piano from Rudolf Serkin.

When I ask the students in my seminar classes what they would like to get from the Inner Game, this issue of 'feeling out of control' often comes up. 'I have always been very nervous in performance,' a student will tell me, 'and this makes me forget my music and play with shaky hands. I hope the Inner Game will allow me to get control of myself so I won't have these problems.'

Students often express the feeling that if they can increase their self-control and make their body do what they want it to do, their problems will be solved.

During a summer workshop in Akron, Ohio, I listened to Janice playing an advanced piano piece by Claude Debussy. The piece was impressionistic, filled with rapid passages creating a delicate texture of rippling sound. Janice was a conservative woman, accustomed to paying careful attention to details. The performance she delivered was very reminiscent of her dress: clean tailored lines, all carefully controlled.

Janice felt her performance lacked dynamic contrast. At my suggestion, she repeated the opening page to find out whether she was observing the printed dynamics. She had indeed missed some altogether and underplayed others. The third time she played it, by heightening her awareness of the dynamics, she was able to bring this element of the piece under her control, and appeared pleased with her performance. Yet there was still something missing.

As an experiment I asked Janice consciously to stop putting the dynamics where they had been marked. Instead, I suggested she should allow her fingers, hands and body to make the decisions for her. Her Self 2 gave a magnificent performance – with brilliant colour, spontaneity and dynamic contrast. The other workshop participants were amazed. So was I.

We were then all stunned to hear that she preferred the first version, when she consciously controlled the dynamics. She said that letting her fingers make spontaneous decisions felt awful. Janice told us that she didn't feel confident of what she was doing, and wasn't able to concentrate on the music at all because it 'seemed to be out of her conscious control'.

She played the piece again and still preferred a sense of conscious control. But the other students unanimously disagreed with her and described the many positive musical changes they had heard when she let her fingers make the choices.

Janice acknowledged that perhaps she wasn't listening as objectively when she surrendered her mental control. She didn't realize that when her fingers made the decisions, she was still completely aware of the music – otherwise her fingers would not have known what to do.

It was a dramatic example of the fact that when Self 1 is busy staying in control and calling all the moves, we can't respond nearly as sensitively to the feelings the music evokes.

Gaining Self 2 control

There's nothing wrong with 'control' itself. And feeling 'out of control' is certainly unpleasant enough to make you tense, thus undermining your experience, performance and even your learning goals for the music. Once again, the solution is simple. Self 1 needs to let go of its control and allow Self 2 to take over.

When Janice was consciously directing her fingers, she felt comfortable because Self 1 was in control – but the music suffered. As she learned to trust Self 2 and began to allow it to take control, she discovered that her fingers 'knew how to play the piece' even better when Self 1 wasn't bombarding them with unnecessary instructions.

We sometimes describe the feeling of Self 2 being in control, quite unfairly, as 'feeling out of control', because from a Self 1 perspective, that's what's happening. Self 1 is no longer in control. But when we sidestep Self 1, our body's wisdom, our instincts and our immediate, intuitive responses come into play, and as a result, Self 2 can be counted on to give a superior performance.

I had the impression that Janice at first felt she couldn't take credit for what happened during this kind of 'Self 2 control'. Her trust was blocked by Self 1's need to feel as though it's in charge of things.

When we trust Self 2 to take over control from Self 1, we are not giving away our trust blindly: we are letting go to years of listening to music and practising the physical movements involved in playing. Our body has stored away memories of every piece we've ever heard, and it responds directly through the nervous system, much faster than Self 1 can respond with a comment such as 'Now make sure your third finger comes down evenly in this run.'

Yehudi Menuhin, the great violinist, once expressed it to me this way: 'Our control is best when we are least aware of it.'

Doubting your own abilities

In the long run, worrying about what others will think and feeling uncomfortable about things getting out of control both boil down to the third of our reasons for blocking trust: we doubt our own inner abilities and musicianship.

Let's take another look at the situation I found myself in when I was playing the Mahler symphony. At some very fundamental level I had lost sight of the most important ingredient: I had forgotten to trust myself.

None of my concerns about my own reputation or that of the Inner Game would have even arisen if I'd simply looked at the piece and remembered that I could play the solo – that I had done it before, I could certainly do it again, and I could probably even play it in my sleep.

The best and worst that could happen

Psychologists have found that one very effective way to deal with worries is to ask oneself, 'What's the worst that could happen, and what would the best possible outcome look like?' When you explore the answers to these questions in a little detail, it usually becomes clear that the 'worst possible case' wouldn't be so bad after all, and that the 'best case' would be just fine – but not so fine that you'd need to worry about it.

The worst thing that could have happened when I was playing the Mahler was that I might have blown the solo. Taking this a little further, perhaps some musicians in other orchestras would have heard about my blunder. The Inner Game might have lost some of its credibility, I suppose, although its reputation doesn't actually all depend on one performance by one musician.

But would I have lost my job? It's unlikely, but not impossible. Could I get another job? Probably. Would my family have disowned me? No. Would the audience, the conductor and my colleagues have forgiven me? I expect so. And would I live through it? Probably.

And what about the best possible outcome? The best thing that could happen in those circumstances was that I would play well and everyone would know it. The audience would be impressed for a moment, until the music picked them up and carried them on to the next crescendo. The conductor would be pleased. Perhaps I'd get a mention in the reviews.

I might pick up some compliments from my colleagues. People would say, 'Nice Mahler, Barry' – but then what? Would I get a rise in salary? Unlikely. And I don't think many people would remember my solo three weeks later.

Why was I so scared, then? I'm a member of a fine symphony orchestra – why should I let my doubts and fears get in the way of the music? Why couldn't I just do what I know how to do – and forget about it?

When I had re-examined the possible consequences of success and failure, and thought about my purpose as a musician, I found I was no longer paralysed by doubt and fear. I was able to trust my experience, my ability and training, and 'let go' and play.

I did fine.

If you find yourself in a situation where you are overcome by your doubts and fears, you may feel unable to focus on your task. But instead of panicking, you can choose one of these two techniques for facing the obstacle before you and getting back in touch with your trust.

Exercise: Reviewing the worst and best that could happen

1. Make a list of the worst outcomes that you could reasonably expect to happen. Include the activity itself, and also its possible consequences.

2. Now list the best outcomes that you could reasonably expect. Again, include the activity itself, and also its possible consequences.

3. Re-examine your purposes and goals, and focus them towards experience and expressing the meaning of the music if that's appropriate.

4. Make a choice to set Self 1's doubts and worries aside, and *trust* that you will survive both the worst and best consequences.

Exercise: The awareness inventory

Taking an inventory of all the things you have going for you can help to restore your trust and confidence. By following the steps below, you can increase your awareness of the skills and abilities you already have:

1. Visual Awareness

Recall how you look when you play the confidence. Allow yourself to run through your store of images that are evoked by the music.

2. Sound Awareness

Remember how the music sounds when you are playing it well. Hear yourself playing it superbly in your head.

3. Feeling Awareness

Recall the way your fingers or throat feels when you're practising. Remember the feelings that the music brings up in you and that you want to express. Be aware of the places in your body where tension sets in and how wonderful it feels to let that tension go.

4. Understanding Awareness

Remember the time you have spent in preparing for this moment. Remember the learnings that you have been through and that your body now 'knows'. Remember the many times when you have played the piece well.

When you have taken inventory of how much you have learned and what you can successfully do, all that remains is for you to *trust* that your abilities will be there when it's time for you to perform.

In the next chapter we will explore a variety of techniques for developing your Inner Game trust skills by letting go and tapping into your real potential as a musician.

Trusting and letting go can feel scary, particularly when there seems to be a lot of pressure on us to perform well. But we seldom accomplish anything really worthwhile without feeling some risk of failure somewhere along the line.

The feeling of risk that comes with trusting and letting go can be a good sign. Over a period of time you may come to recognize it as a signal that you're about to let go and let Self 2 take over.

It's understandable if we refuse our trust to something that fails us, that doesn't deliver what it promises. But Self 2 deserves to be trusted because it proves how trustworthy it is over and over again. And that's one of the great benefits of consciously playing the Inner Game: the more you let Self 2 go through its paces, the clearer it becomes just how trustworthy and talented Self 2 really is.

Trust must be present before we can let go to Self 2 and perform at our best. But when we trust Self 2, we're not trusting blindly – we're trusting the most capable part of ourselves. Whom would you rather trust? Self 1 is trying to sabotage your playing. Self 2 is the real musician.

7 Letting go

The way people fall asleep is a perfect illustration of Inner Game principles at work. Falling alseep is something you 'know how to do' and yet can't do deliberately when your conscious mind is running a mile a minute.

Sure, you can feel tired, know that it's time to sleep, and put yourself in bed. Then if 'there's nothing on your mind', you'll be able to fall asleep without making any special effort; it will happen naturally. But what about those times when your head is full of a thousand details or worries?

The nagging voice of Self 1 can be enough to keep anyone awake. And it doesn't always stop at telling us about tomorrow's problems or running a quick inventory of the day that's just past. Sometimes it takes a hand in the business of falling asleep itself. 'You aren't really tired yet; you won't be able to get to sleep,' it tells us. Or 'I know you're exhausted, but there are still a number of problems we haven't resolved and you'll never get to sleep while you're thinking so much.' Or 'Go to sleep. Go on. Sleep! *Relax*! Close your eyes, stop wiggling your feet and *Lie still*!' The great problem with going to sleep is that as long as you're trying to do it, you can't.

As you might expect, the secret of getting to sleep when Self 1 is holding the floor is to use an awareness exercise. Counting sheep is a classic awareness exercise for falling asleep, and there are many others. Have you ever used the technique of simply paying attention to your breathing? Closed your eyes and imagined a black space with a white dot in the middle? Picked up a book and read it until you fell asleep over the pages? Or counted to a hundred, or a thousand, or until you simply couldn't count anymore because you were . . . sound asleep?

The purpose of all these techniques is to deflect your attention from Self 1 and allow Self 2 to fall asleep (which it knows perfectly well how to do).

Three phases of falling asleep

There are three phases to falling asleep using one of these techniques. Let's explore them:

● First, you notice that Self 1 is interfering with your wishes and realize you need to 'quiet your mind'. You make a conscious decision to put your awareness on something other than the restless inner talk of Self 1.

● Next, you focus on something simple, such as counting sheep or watching the regular ebb and flow of your breathing. This takes your attention away from Self 1's doubts and instructions, which then begin to fade away.

● Finally, you 'let go'. You are no longer trying to control the situation, Self 2 takes over, and you fall asleep.

How much do you remember about falling asleep? Have you ever managed to get to sleep by ordering yourself to do it? Is it something you can make happen, or does sleep somehow always 'come over you while you're not looking' – in a unique way of its own? Do you ever remember the precise moment when you fell asleep? Or only the drowsy moment just before it?

We rarely doubt our ability to get to sleep. We know it's something we can 'do' when we 'let it happen'. But we also admit that the actual moment of letting go and falling asleep is outside our conscious control.

Giving yourself to the music

Whether we're simply trying to go to sleep or trying to tap into the musicality of Self 2, letting go of Self 1's litany of doubts, fears, suggestions, corrections and concepts of what will work is not always an easy business. Self 1 fights to keep our attention.

When we're playing music, Self 1 wants to instruct us,

correct us, and generally inform us why we shouldn't trust Self 2. This leaves us with a widening gap between what we feel inside, and what Self 1 is telling us. We need to build up our confidence and learn to trust that there is something within us that can discover and perform from resources that go way beyond our conscious mind.

Letting go finally happens when we can give up conscious control and allow ourselves to receive and transmit the musicianship of Self 2. We may still play some part in channelling Self 2's musicianship, but at some very fundamental level letting go means letting go of our conscious control of what is going on, and this is what gives our music spontaneity, and power.

That's where the real control – Self 2 control – comes in.

Eight ways of letting go

I have found eight techniques that can help musicians to let go of Self 1 concepts and tap into the superior abilities of Self 2. I'd like to encourage you to explore, change or extend these techniques in whatever ways work best for you.

In the rest of this chapter we shall explore each of the eight techniques for 'letting go' in more detail. I'd encourage you to do all the exercises in this chapter, substituting your own repertoire for the musical examples if you like.

It's quite possible that Self 1 will tell you that you don't need to do all the exercises, that you know better ways of going about things, that the exercises won't work for you, and that some of them are ridiculous. Some of the exercises are designed to be ridiculous, and in fact your very unwillingness is a sign that you have a normally functioning Self 1. If you didn't feel any reluctance in attempting these exercises, you might not be successfully letting go.

Letting go is a sometimes embarrassing, scary and difficult process. But until you can pass through the temporary barrier of your embarrassment, you won't have the opportunity to discover what Self 2 has to offer you. So take the plunge, do the exercises, let go – and discover what's waiting for you on the other side.

Technique 1: role playing

Mary, a viola player, played a slow sarabande by Bach during a presentation Tim Gallwey and I made at the Music Educators National Conference in San Antonio, Texas. The piece requires sustained control of the bow arm, a warm tone and precise pitch. Mary was noticeably self-conscious playing before this large gathering of educators. She had difficulty keeping her bow from shaking, and her tone was thin and scratchy.

Both Tim and I could see that Mary had a warm feeling for the music she was playing but that she felt too inhibited to express it.

Tim spoke to Mary privately for a few moments so that the audience wouldn't know what instruction he had given her. He asked her who her favourite Bach viola player was, and she replied that it was Martha Katz. Tim then instructed her to imagine there was a video camera above the stage taping her performance. He told Mary it didn't matter whether she played out of tune or missed notes or had poor tone. All that mattered was that she should look the way Martha Katz looked while playing Bach. He told her the camera was only recording the way she looked, and that her sound would be replaced by a tape of Martha Katz playing the same piece.

Since Mary no longer had to worry about how she played, she felt free to throw herself into the role of Martha Katz during the mock taping session. She not only looked confident, relaxed and dignified – she also played with bow control, accuracy and fine phrasing. She effectively 'became' Martha Katz as she performed the Bach sarabande.

The audience was stunned by her playing and curious to know what instructions Tim had given her that had produced such a marked effect. And Mary realized that although she had been imagining she was Martha Katz, she was still the one playing the viola.

Tim first developed this 'role-playing' technique in *The Inner Game of Tennis*, where he suggested that timid and awkward players can often change their attitude and their tennis by pretending to play like John McEnroe or Chris Evert Lloyd. Musicians can enjoy the same immediate shift in attitude and results by pretending to be their own favourite virtuoso performers – Rostropovich or Rampal, Sills or Sinatra.

Exercise: Role playing

The idea of this exercise is to allow yourself access to more of your hidden musicianship by playing the way your favourite performer plays.

1. Play or sing a piece of your own choosing, trying to get every note exactly as it ought to be. If you're a classical player, you might play the melody line from Mozart's Sonata in C.

If you're a singer, you might sing the first half of 'White Christmas'.

2. Now do it again, this time pretending you are one of your favourite performers, your teacher – or yourself, ten years from now. You don't have to play all the notes correctly; just play *as if* you were the performer of your choice. If you sang 'White Christmas', pretend you're Bing Crosby this time, and give it all the relaxed warmth that he might give it.

Did you notice a difference? Did you find yourself expressing musical qualities that you wouldn't normally expect?

Technique 2: becoming the music

Losing yourself in a character you are portraying musically, or in the emotions of the music, is another way of letting go. I met Ryan Edwards when he was performing the baritone role of Billy Bigelow in a Cincinnati Opera production of *Carousel*. I asked him about the acting course for singers that he conducts, and he told me that most singers are so preoccupied with their vocal cords that it's hard for them to act – at first. 'But then a funny thing happens,' he told me. 'The more they begin to get into their character, the better they sing.'

If you are to perform the role of the devil in Gounod's

SONATA No. 1 in C MAJOR

W. A. Mozart

Moderately fast

(Voice) la   la   la   *etc.*

opera *Faust*, the chances are that you will be more convincing if you pretend to be the devil than if you simply imitate your favourite bass-baritone. Barbra Streisand's historic performance in *Funny Girl* came from her ability to become – in body, mind and spirit – the character of Fanny Brice.

Adrienne, a soprano, not only improved her performance by 'becoming' the character she was portraying – she was also able to perform without self-consciousness, and without her back troubling her as it often did.

'When I began singing the "Grandmother's Lullaby" from Menotti's *The Consul*,' she told me, 'I was very concerned about my performance and tensed up my back and shoulder muscles as a result, which meant that I couldn't breathe freely. It was very difficult to portray an elderly woman singing this soft, caressing melody, when my body felt as though I'd been lifting weights all morning.

'I decided to eliminate the pressure that I felt singing in front of a group by focusing on the character of the old lady. We turned out the lights, and I sat slumped in a chair for a few minutes. Then I began just speaking the text of the song as though I was an old woman. I found myself reaching into the darkness for my imaginary child, and discovered I was very close to tears.

'When the lights came on again, I felt peaceful and assured. I knew I had become the old woman, and my sense of myself as a singer had disappeared. The tension was gone, my fear of poor articulation and intonation was gone, all my work-related phobias and fears had vanished. The music flowed through me . . .'

Exercise: Becoming the music

1. Sing or play each of the four excerpts that follow. Only focus on the pitches, rhythm and printed markings. Ignore the 'meaning' of each piece.

2. Now repeat each excerpt, this time forgetting about the notes or your instrument, and allowing your personality to merge with the meaning of each piece. You *become* the music (the parent, the elephant, the anger, the swan).

CRADLE SONG

Slow to moderate
(tenderly)

J. Brahms

Lull - a - by and good night, Ro - ses co - ver my child___ ti - ny spark - les round your head and___ slip in - to the bed.

CARNIVAL of the ANIMALS

Moderate
(robustly)

C. Saint-Saëns

(Voice) da da da *etc.*

Moderate to fast
(trem.) *(trem.)* *(trem.)*

(Voice) ta ta ta ta *etc.*

CARNIVAL of the ANIMALS

Slowly
(expressively)

C. Saint-Saëns

(Voice) la la la *etc.*

Exercise: Listening for character

Play a recording of a tone poem by Strauss (*Till Eulenspiegel* or *Don Juan*), or the Berlioz *Symphonie Fantastique*. Listen for character. See if you can hear the different themes. What is the 'personality' of each phrase?

Do you hear playfulness? Excitement? Love? A ball? A hanging?

Technique 3: doing something familiar

This technique for letting go is similar to the idea of 'the Doctrine of the Easy' which we discussed in Chapter 3. The task is to associate your musical challenges with other activities that are easy and familiar. The simpler the activity, and the further it's removed from any musical associations, the higher the chance you have of the technique working.

During the winter of 1983, I had the privilege of making a presentation to approximately sixty bass players in Peking, China. My lecture had to be given through an interpreter, and I was not entirely sorry to realize that I could only communicate the simplest thoughts in this way. This was no time for me to be giving out complex technical instructions.

A young bass player performed a solo by Koussevitsky. He was having difficulty sustaining an even tone with his bow. At first I felt like going into a detailed explanation of the arm movement that is required for smoothness of tone. Since that wasn't possible, I asked him if he and the other musicians present ever went fishing. The response was instantaneous – big smiles from all around me. But what did my question have to do with the tone of a double bass?

I explained that sustaining an even tone on the bass is like keeping a fish on the line: if there is slack in the line, the fish will be able to jerk its way free. The resistance in the line must be maintained while you reel the fish in. My instruction to the bass player was to continue to play the melody while maintaining the tension in the bow. When he felt the resistance was becoming too strong or too weak, he was to adjust his bow to keep it constant.

The bass student took up his bow in a way that suggested 'I

know exactly how to do it now', and he made it look easy: his bow tension was even, and his tone full and resonant. When I learned that the entire party would be out fishing that afternoon for their evening meal, I understood those smiles – and the ease with which the student had picked up on my instruction.

Lois was having trouble playing the triplets – three equal notes spread over the space of two notes – in her piano version of the *Chariots of Fire* theme. She found herself repeatedly playing two quick notes followed by a longer one. The class made a number of suggestions, but none of them seemed to do the trick.

It occurred to me that we needed an easy and familiar cue to give her the sense of the rhythm she needed. It also occurred to me that it was a hot day and I was getting hungry. I thought about ice cream: maybe I should go get some after the class. Mocha almond fudge? Chocolate chocolate chip? No – I've got it: *pineapple*.

'Pineapple,' I said to Lois. 'Ice cream. After class?' She perked up considerably. 'Now back to the triplets. "Pine-apple" is a word where all three syllables have a rather equal duration. Every time you get to one of the triplets, I want you to sing the word "pine-apple" out loud as you play the three notes.'

It worked. When Lois substituted her appreciative under-standing of the rhythm (and implications) of the word 'pine-apple' for her confusion about the triplets, she had no problem playing the three notes evenly. There was even something delicious and cool about the way she played that afternoon.

Exercise: Doing something familiar

For Wind Players. Play the passage below the way you have been taught to play it.

(Voice) pah   pah   pah   pah

Now repeat the passage, but instead of focusing on the articulation you have been taught, imagine that with each note you are blowing out the candles on a birthday cake.

For String Players. Play the passage below with an 'off-the-string' spiccato motion.

(Voice) Bing Bing Bing Bing *etc.*

Now repeat the passage, but insted of focusing on the bow motion, play with the centre or lower part of the bow, and imagine you are bouncing a basketball (the tip of the bow represents the ball). As you play each note, say the word 'bing' as the bow bounces off the string.

For Keyboard. Play the passage with a staccato motion.

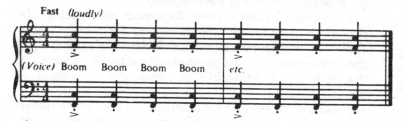

(Voice) Boom Boom Boom Boom *etc.*

Now repeat, this time imagining your hands are beating a tribal drum. Don't worry about missing the notes. Say the word 'boom' as you play each chord.

For Voice. Sing the melody of the Hallelujah chorus from Handel's *Messiah* as you have been taught.

THE MESSIAH

G. Handel

Hal - le - lu - jah, Hal - le - lu - jah, Hal-le - lu-jah, Hal-le-lu-jah,

Repeat the passage, but instead of trying to sing correctly, imagine that you are laughing, and that the "Hal-le-lu-jah" is a deep laugh breaking out of you and projecting all the way to the back of a huge auditorium.

Technique 4: letting the body take over

On my Pacific tour I coached Edith, a bass player from the New Zealand Symphony. She had tried to use her vibrato in a number of different places in a slow, expressive sonata by Vivaldi and couldn't decide where it 'worked' best. None of her experiments quite had the right feel to them.

I wanted Edith to discover the best places for vibrato by herself, so I asked her to play the piece without making any effort to put in a vibrato. I asked her to imagine that her fingers, not her brain, would tell her what to do, and suggested that she only use vibrato when her fingers 'screamed at her' to do so. Since she would not have decided in advance which notes needed the vibrato, I was confident that her hands would be free to supply it unconsciously.

Her performance improved immediately: both her sound and her vibrato were smoother and richer. Edith was a little shocked to discover that she could actually feel messages from her hands. She played another passage and said, 'This time I want to ask my hands about phrasing. If I can stay out of the way, they may be able to teach me more than I knew that I knew!'

I remember another occasion, where a different kind of 'letting go by letting the body take over' helped. A bassoonist came to a class I was teaching, bringing four pieces with her. She wasn't sure which one she wanted to play and was picking up first one and then another, and she obviously was concerned not to make 'the wrong choice'.

I asked her not to make any decision, but to ask her fingers and body what they would like to do. She laughed at first and then felt herself reaching out for one particular piece. It wasn't the right choice by any particular set of logical rules – 'the most difficult, so that I have the most challenge', or 'the easiest, so I don't make a fool of myself', or anything like that. But it was the right choice at a much deeper level.

It was right for her at that precise moment.

Exercise: Letting the body take over

1. Sing or play the spiritual 'Swing Low, Sweet Chariot'. Notice your use of vibrato.

SWING LOW, SWEET CHARIOT

Slowly   Spiritual

Swing low, sweet char - i - ot, __ Com-ing for to car - ry me

home.   Swing __ low,   sweet   char - i - ot, __

Com - ing   for   to   car - ry   me   home.

2. Now repeat the passage, but do not use any vibrato.

3. Repeat the passage again, this time allowing yourself to vibrate on the notes that 'demand' warmth and a vibrating sound. It may be easier for you to do this if you put your attention on the part of your body that is responsible for producing vibrato. Invite your body to communicate its sense of the music to you, and then co-operate with it.

Did you notice any difference between the first and third readings? Did you choose to vibrate on different notes the third time around? Did you use more vibrato, or less?

Exercise: Letting your body choose the music

The next time you practise, instead of playing your usual warm-ups – etudes, solos, etc. – invite your body (arms, fingers, throat, abdomen) to choose what it feels like playing. Follow the direction your feelings give you, at least for this one practice session.

After your practice, ask yourself whether you learned more

or less, played better or worse, and felt more or less musically involved than usual. Does 'choosing your music by feel' improve the quality of your practice?

Technique 5: letting go to the environment

Another way to let go of Self 1 worries and gain access to your Self 2 musicianship is by 'letting go to the environment'. What we mean is that you can use your environment to trigger Self 2 perceptions.

Alan told me he wanted to improve his playing of the famous Schubert *Arpeggione Sonata* on the cello, which he felt lacked brightness, precision, softness and overall energy. I suggested he might like to experiment with 'letting go to the environment'.

First, we looked around the room to find objects that had some of the qualities Alan felt were lacking in his playing. Someone noticed the chrome borders on the windows, and remarked that they were bright, straight, precise and glistening. I asked Alan to look at the chrome for a minute and then play the passage as if he embodied the spirit of the chrome. His music immediately took on a noticeable precision and brightness.

We were inspired by the success of this first attempt and started looking round the room to find something that was both translucent and complex. The plastic grid covering the fluorescent lights in the classroom ceiling fitted the bill: it seemed to be made of thousands of tiny translucent squares that diffused the light and somewhat softened the effect of the long fluorescent bulbs.

I asked Alan to imagine this sparkling translucent grid talking to him. 'I am perfect,' the screen seemed to say, 'and am composed of many thousands of equal parts. I am translucent, moulding the harsh light that comes through me into a softer, smoother texture. I am strong but flexible.' I asked Alan to play the solo again, this time expressing the qualities he had found in the light grid. Again, the results were immediate.

Next, we looked for something with a distinctly soft quality. The beige cotton curtains in the room hung down in gentle curves and folds that were in marked contrast to the hard lines of the chrome and plastic fixtures. Once again, Alan was able to play the piece in a way which exhibited the desired quality.

Finally, Alan played the piece again, this time integrating all the expressive values that had been triggered in him by the chrome, the plastic grid and the curtains. By letting the objects in the room trigger in him the qualities that he felt were lacking in his playing, Alan had found a new source of inspiration for his music and thus avoided the concerns and worries of Self 1.

Exercise: Letting go to the environment

1. Sing, play or listen to 'America the Beautiful'.

AMERICA, the BEAUTIFUL

Moderately   Samuel A. Ward

O beau-ti-ful for spa-cious skies, For am-ber waves of grain, For pur-ple moun-tain maj-es-ties A-bove the fruit-ed plain.

2. Look outside the window (or around your room) for scenes and objects that can trigger a deeper experience of the meaning of the lyrics. *Beautiful*. What do you see that triggers a sense of beauty in you? A flower? A painting? The play of light and shade? Study the object that arouses this sense of beauty in you. Immerse yourself in it. Pretend you are the object, and describe what is beautiful about yourself. Try talking to the flower, the painting, the shadows and the pools of light. Ask them what they can teach you about the music.

When you have deepened your feeling for the word *beautiful*, repeat the process with *spacious, skies, amber, grain, purple, mountain* and so on.

3. Play, sing or listen to 'America the Beautiful' again. If you are playing an instrument, you can vary your tone,

attacks, dynamics, pulse and vibrato to express your feelings about these key words. This time, how effective were you in experiencing and communicating the meaning of the song?

Did you notice any difference in your level of involvement in the music? How did your playing change?

Technique 6: letting go to overload

I discovered this technique more or less by accident while I was teaching a class of adult beginners. Adults who take up an instrument sometimes have a particularly hard time of it because they're used to listening to recordings of the great virtuosos. When they listen to their own early steps, they often compare themselves unfavourably (and unfairly) with Jean-Pierre Rampal or James Galway. In order to make sure these students simply wouldn't have any attention left over to worry about how they sounded, I decided to overload their senses and their brains. I was completely unprepared for the results.

If someone had told me that a person with no previous experience of the instrument could be taught to play 'Mary Had a Little Lamb' on the bass with a full sound and correct position while smiling, singing the words and directing the audience to sing along – all in the first fifteen minutes – I simply wouldn't have believed them. No one could possibly remember that much.

But I watched it happen. When you short-circuit the mind by giving it an 'overload' of things to deal with, it has so many things to attend to that it no longer has time to worry. Self 1 sometimes 'checks out', and lets Self 2 'check in'.

I asked John, a clarinetist who was taking my beginner's bass class in Akron, Ohio, to play the bass, sing, conduct – and make it all look effortless. I showed him a comfortable playing position, demonstrating it for him without giving him verbal instructions. When I noticed his hand was in an awkward position, I pointed to my own hand for comparison and showed him a position that involved less tension on the wrist. I asked him whether he was comfortable and told him to mention any tension or discomfort to me as soon as he noticed it.

John learned to draw the bow by watching me draw my own. He could feel the resistance of the hair pulling against the strings and maintained it by pretending to 'keep the fish on the line'. He found he didn't need to look at his bow, because his arm could sense the resistance and his ear told him whether his sound was consistent.

I sang and played 'Mary Had a Little Lamb' and asked John to sing it and play it along with me. Since the tune was easy, singing didn't interfere with his playing. Rather than asking him to 'conduct' the class with his head – which might have seemed a rather complex and distracting business – I asked him to 'give the words to the audience' by bobbing his head with each syllable.

Finally, I asked him to express the fun he was obviously having with the rest of us. I suggested he could do this by laughing or smiling, or just by projecting a carefree, happy-go-lucky attitude with his shoulders. I encouraged him to feel comfortable, jump in, trust himself and enjoy it.

What I didn't tell John was that what he would be attempting would normally be considered out of the question for a beginner. And I didn't give him time to think about it and come to that conclusion for himself, either.

There just wasn't any problem. John performed effortlessly – and the class was amazed. When we asked him how he had managed to pull off so many different tasks at the same time, he said he didn't know.

It is helpful to know that when we are faced with an overwhelming barrage of tasks, this kind of short-circuit is likely to happen. We can recognize the situation and quickly choose to give up 'trying'. The sooner we let go, and trust the Self 2 musician inside us, the sooner our performance will improve.

My students have often told me that once they learned to recognize 'overload' and let go to it, they were able to avoid panicking and could handle situations that would have previously left them confused, frustrated, and tense.

Sometimes a conductor or teacher may give you so many 'do instructions' at one time that you feel completely overloaded. There are just too many things to think about for you to keep them all in your head at one time. When this happens, the secret is just to listen to the instructions. Don't think you have to follow all these instructions consciously; let go, and let Self 2 handle them.

Exercise: Letting go to overload

1. Play a piece that you're working on at the moment and notice the areas that you feel need more attention.

2. Imagine that your teacher or a conductor is overloading you with instructions. Make a list of four or five helpful instructions that you might receive about the piece: something about a difficult fingering passage, something about your tone, something about playing up to tempo, something about the dynamics and so on – and when you have a list of 'things to work on' that seems far too much to handle all at once, simply read the list through to yourself.

3. Forget about your list, and play the piece.

Did you find that Self 2 had somehow managed to deal with several or all of the problem areas – without any deliberate effort on your part?

Next time you feel you are being given an 'instruction overload' during a lesson or rehearsal, simply listen to the instructions, don't worry about them, let go of them, and play the piece. Anytime you feel you're getting close to being 'overloaded', you can save yourself a lot of panic if you recognize it as a signal to let go to Self 2.

Technique 7: letting go to the ridiculous

When Tim Gallwey is coaching tennis players, he sometimes asks them to 'play tennis the way you imagine a fish would play', or to 'play like a bird'. He finds this exercise works particularly well for players who are usually concerned to 'look good' while they play. By inviting them to look ridiculous, he allows them to let go of their Self 1 image of themselves so that Self 2 can get on with the job of playing tennis. It often seems as though Tim's 'fish' pupils play a whole lot better than they did as 'serious players'.

Classical musicians often feel they have a 'serious image' to keep up, and one way to break out of any tendency you may have to act (and play) like a stuffed shirt is deliberately to set yourself a ridiculous task and let go to it.

Last year I performed Jon Deak's 'The Ugly Duckling' for soprano and string quartet. It's a 'theatre piece', and I had to wear a duck costume for the first movement and a huge swan's head for the second. Playing the double bass while wearing a duck costume was something new to me; I'm more used to performing in white tie and tails. I let go to the ridiculous – and began to enjoy myself immensely.

But worse was to come. Since the swan's head towered a full four feet above my head, I had to look out of my costume through a white screen hidden among the neck feathers. I hadn't memorized the music for the concert, which was being broadcast live on TV. I had practised it, and I could read the score and play it, but I didn't know it by heart. Then disaster struck: my shoulder strap broke, and the swan's neck slipped down so I could no longer see my bass, the music, the soprano or the quartet. Since nobody knew that I had suddenly 'gone blind', the music went on – and I had to play.

You might say I faked it. I missed a number of notes, to be sure, but having already let go to the ridiculous, I found I needed to let go again. This time I 'let go to the impossible' (Technique 8 on the list of strategies for letting go, which we will dicusss in detail after this one) – and was surprised by how much my body and hands remembered.

Exercise: Letting go to the ridiculous

You may resist doing this exercise. When you read through the instructions, you may hear Self 1 making comments such as 'This is ridiculous. It's beneath my dignity. And it's impossible in any case.' Good. That's the way Self 1 should have felt. Self 1's need to feel 'in control', its wish not to be embarrassed or insulted and its fear of failure are all natural blocks to letting go. But until you get past these blocks, you'll never know what Self 2 is capable of.

That's what this exercise is all about. Frankly, it is a bit ridiculous. And it is complex enough to be virtually impossible without Self 2 input. It can teach you how to trust and let go, and what the benefits of that trust can be.

If you saw the movie *Amadeus*, you probably remember the party scene in which Mozart has to pay a forfeit. Several men pick him up and carry him on his back to a keyboard, which he plays with his hands bent back behind his head. Mozart, who has shown himself to be something of a Punk kid throughout the movie, doesn't feel embarrassed in the least to be playing in this way – in fact, he plays pretty well.

1. If you sing or play a small, portable instrument, lie down on your back on the floor. If you play a keyboard instrument, turn the bench so that it's perpendicular to the instrument and lie down along it on your stomach, so that your head is below the keyboard but you can still reach the keys.

GREENSLEEVES

2. Now play the melody 'Greensleeves' from memory.

3. Repeat it in a jazz style – change the rhythm, add variations, triplets, etc. If you have never played jazz before, that's a plus: you can begin to explore the medium. If you play jazz already, pick another style that you have never tried: Baroque, Romantic, avantgarde or any other style you choose. While you are playing, let your feet dance in the air (gently; don't overtax those stomach muscles). If you play a keyboard instrument, hum along with the melody.

Did you hear Self 1 trying to persuade you not to do the exercise? Did you do it anyway? How did that feel? What

121

about your playing? Did you manage it? Did you enjoy yourself? What did you play that surprised you? What did you discover you could do that you wouldn't have thought you could do unless you'd seen it? What did you learn about yourself? About your instrument?

Technique 8: letting go to the impossible

During one of my tennis lessons with Tim Gallwey, he asked me to do something 'impossible'. He asked me to stand at the net and give my best effort to reaching every shot he hit at me. He warned me in advance that the balls would be coming high and wide – and fast – and told me I couldn't possibly hit them. But he wanted me to try for them.

Tim hit the first ball over my head and over the fence behind me. I didn't move a muscle. 'I want you to go for every shot,' he told me. 'Those are the instructions. OK?' I said OK, but when the next ball sailed way over on the other side of the court, I made a token gesture of reaching for it with my racket.

'Barry, I'd like you to forget about getting your racket to the ball. You're not going to be able to reach a single one of these shots. All I want you to do is to make the maximum possible effort in each case, even knowing that you aren't going to be able to reach the ball. Have fun, and go for it.'

'OK,' I told myself, 'this time I'll show Tim I can jump for the clouds if necessary.' The ball came whizzing over the net and I leapt from the ground with a twisting backhand. I had no intention of reaching the ball, but somehow if found the edge of my racket. I was amazed.

When you have no intention of succeeding, but 'let go to the impossible', impossible things sometimes happen. Once again, I'm not recommending that you should get yourself into impossible circumstances for the sake of it. But I am suggesting that 'letting go to the impossible' is often a fruitful approach in times of crisis.

'Letting go to the impossible' isn't something you necessarily have to keep in reserve until you get stuck in a swan's throat in the middle of a performance, though. In fact, it's a technique you can also use quite deliberately to vary the tempo at which you learn a 'fast' piece.

Nick was learning a Bach two-part invention on the piano. The piece involves playing flurries of semi-quavers in rapid succession. Usually, a student would begin by learning to play the piece carefully at a slower tempo. Only after several months of getting the fingers and muscles used to the piece would he or she attempt to play it at a faster pace.

Nick had just reached the point where he knew which fingerings worked best for him. He was playing the piece steadily, with good control, and monitoring his movements carefully. When I asked him if he had ever played it 'up to tempo', he gave me a look and asked me, 'Are you kidding? I've only been playing the piece a few weeks.' Unabashed, I said, 'Let's pretend you've played it for a few months, and see what it feels like to play it fast.'

'I won't be able to keep track of the notes without having memorized them,' Nick told me. 'It's impossible.' Then we grinned at each other, and he picked up the challenge. He tried the piece at the 'impossible' tempo and amazed us both by making only a few small mistakes. 'I couldn't believe I was playing that fast – and so accurately,' he told me. 'When I realized what was happening, I forced myself to make some mistakes so I wouldn't feel out of control. But I admit it. The impossible seems to be possible.'

'Letting go to the impossible' is a neat name for this approach, but it's not really very accurate. What this exercise is really about is letting go to the possible. It's a matter of letting go to a potential that each one of us has within us but that we haven't been giving ourselves credit for.

Exercise: Letting go to the impossible

1. Play or sing (using syllables like 'ta-ka, ta-ka') the following lines, at a slow enough tempo that you feel sure you can be accurate. It doesn't matter how slow the tempo is – just make sure you can get the notes right. Do this until you feel fairly comfortable with the notes.

2. You are playing Rimsky-Korsakov's 'Flight of the Bumblebee'. The tempo should be so fast that the notes blur into the buzz of a bee. Now repeat the piece; but this time play it five or six times faster. Don't worry about getting the notes right this time, just go for the impossible – at high speed. Go at it with reckless abandon. *Buzz*.

What happened? Did you manage more of the notes than you'd expected? Did it sound more or less like a bumblebee? Did you really let go when you played the second time? If you didn't, if you hesitated, or got caught up in Self 1, play the piece again, until you feel the delicious out-of-control sensation you sometimes get when you're running downhill.

Did you enjoy it?

8 Coping with obstacles

Before the concert Cynthia tried every Inner Game technique she knew to quiet the nagging voice of Self 1. She focused on the score, the sound of her playing, the emotions in the music and her knowledge about it. She clarified her musical goals in the areas of performance, experience and learning, tried playing as if she were Rampal, and practised every trust exercise I had ever suggested. Nothing worked.

Finally, in complete frustration she stopped trying to make the techniques work for her and concentrated the full force of her attention on the bald spot on her teacher's head as he sat there in the front row of the audience.

Self 1 disappeared.

'Barry,' she told me after the concert, 'that wasn't fair. You never told me "focusing on the bald spot" was the most powerful awareness technique in the book.'

Continual Creativity

Cynthia's story illustrates an important point: yesterday's inventive and successful technique is stale today, in much the same way that yesterday's successful interpretation is today's repeat performance. Certainly, we should be aware of the feeling and phrasing of a fine performance, but we should build on them, so that each performance is literally a re-creation of the music.

I find that playing the Inner Game demands continual creativity. The techniques of the Inner Game are designed to slip you past the obstacles that stand between you and your musicality, but when you become 'devoted' to a particular technique instead of the music, the technique can lose its effectiveness.

Every moment provides you with a new opportunity to play the Inner Game.

You will need to make new choices and take new and different directions in your approach to music if your performance is to improve. Change is not something we ordinarily relish. The motivation for continual change can only come from experiencing the improvement in your music that occurs when you set realistic goals and trust the musician within you. Your challenge is to recognize the opportunities for appropriate change that the Inner Game offers you and to be responsive to them. The quicker you can recognize your old patterns and adopt a strategy for sidestepping them, the sooner you will be free of indecision, doubt and fear – free to play music.

This chapter will showcase some of the many ways in which Inner Game students have used appropriate techniques in the context of musical performance. The first part of the chapter will explore choices and decisions that can help you to sidestep mental interference. In the second part we shall explore ways to deal with external obstacles. You may be handling inner interference perfectly and playing like a master – until your colleagues or your accompanist, a sudden equipment failure or some other unpredictable occurrence 'throws you for a loop' in the course of a performance. You need to be prepared for the unexpected, and again, that requires constant creativity and alterness.

Dealing with Internal Interference

Whenever I run across an orchestral colleague, student, or friend who brings up the topic of 'mental obstacles', I begin by challenging myself to discover which area – awareness, will or trust – seems to be most out of balance. Sometimes, of course, all three areas need attention, but it is important to be patient and explore one thing at a time. When I have a sense of which area needs the most work or should be dealt with first, I know where to set my goal and can begin to suggest alternative courses of action that might be of help.

Of course, this process of identifying a goal and suggesting alternative strategies becomes much easier with practice. The 'fishing line' analogy with bow tension worked wonderfully with my Chinese friends because they fished for their supper. But it has worked for others, too, and the longer I play the Inner Game, the greater my store of successful ploys and devices becomes.

In this chapter, then, I want to share many of the specific applications of Inner Game principles that I have used, but also to suggest that your own sensitivity, intuition and creativity will allow you to rephrase these approaches in ways that more exactly fit your own situation.

You are a musician, a creative artist and your peak performance will draw on everything you have learned, everything you know 'deep in your bones' – and on the inspiration of the moment.

Let's explore some of the ways in which the Inner Game skills of awareness, will and trust can be used to cope with internal interference.

Will skills

Ellen panicked before her final exam. She lost her usual confidence in her singing and came to me for some last minute help. 'What am I going to do?' she asked me. 'I know I'm going to fail this exam.'

Not surprisingly, right before one of the most crucial exams in her life, she was concerned about results, and her nervousness had made her lose touch with her love of music. I wanted to help her refocus her attention, away from her worries and back on to the experience of the music itself, so I asked her why she wanted to be a singer in the first place. 'Because I love it,' she told me, 'but, Barry, I'm not loving it now.'

I asked Ellen about the song she was singing, and at first she didn't want to talk about it. She turned the conversation back to her nervousness, her fear of failing, and kept asking me for techniques. 'Tell me about the song.' It was hard for her at that moment, but she told me. She told me about the meaning of the song, its general background, its lyrical quality. Something changed inside her as she spoke. I could sense her love for the music returning, and with it her confidence. 'Have you prepared the piece thoroughly?' I asked. 'And can you convey the feelings that you've described for me?' 'Thanks, Barry – and yes, I know the piece inside out. And I love to sing.'

Ellen told her classmates later that she left her anxieties in the snack bar, and sang for her exam. She focused on the lyrical qualities of the song, and the music was wonderful. That's all she could remember about the performance. She forgot to ask whether she'd passed or failed. She passed – with honours.

Refocusing on your original musical goals can work wonders – and can help you to sidestep your mental obstacles in the process. It's something that you can learn from the examples in this book, or with the help of an Inner Game coach, but it's also a skill that you need to develop by practice and carry with you into those all important performance situations.

A horn player once described to me how he avoided sabotaging an important concert. 'I was playing an exposed solo in the Brahms Double Concerto with the Philharmonic,' he told me. 'I got through it just well enough to get away with it – but I was a nervous wreck. I asked myself why I was feeling like such a jerk, and what the point of it all was. And then I began to think about music, and remembered why I had become a musician in the first place. I began to listen to the grand sweep of the music, and by the time my next entrance came around, I knew why I loved Brahms so much. I played with all the feeling and skill I'm capable of – and it was marvellous.'

Awareness skills

Jackie, a harpist, described to one of my classes how she used awareness techniques to draw her concentration away from her anxiety and concern to play accurately, and focus it on the music. 'I'd been practising during a break in an orchestral rehearsal,' she told us, 'when a voice behind me said, "Don't be nervous." I turned around and saw it was Barry Green. Now if there's one remark in the world that might be calculated to make you nervous, that's it. I told myself Barry was crazy if he thought he would manage to get me off balance.

'Just before my entrance, that voice was there again: "Don't shake," it said, "I'm back here watching every move." Barry was grinning like a kid who knows he's being bad, and I told myself, "He's nuts – I'm not going to be nervous."

'The possibility was there, though, so I decided to make use of the opportunity to use what I'd learned about awareness. I began to go through the way I wanted my part to sound, and mentally explored how the strings would feel when I played my glissandos. And I paid special attention to what was going on in other sections of the orchestra.

'Barry was a little devious, but he really made me put my awareness techniques to the test. I was delighted to find I was able to concentrate on one thing at a time – and the techniques worked.'

As Jason, a young violinist, walked on stage to play a concerto, he found he was in a total panic. He decided to focus on the pianist's introduction, and listened so intently that he began to discover new sounds in the concerto. 'When it was my time to play,' he told us, 'I was eager to get involved. I had forgotten about the audience, and where my desperation went I never knew.'

Trust skills

Charles, a cellist, found himself feeling very nervous before a concerto performance. 'I really felt that I knew the piece very well,' he told us, 'but somehow I kept allowing Self 1 to cast doubts on my ability. About half an hour before the performance I realized I was letting Self 1 interfere and that I needed to get beyond it in order to play. I decided to forget I was a student in a competition and to imagine being Lynn Harrell for a day.

'I brushed my hair aside, strode out on stage feeling confident and proud, and enjoyed every minute of my dual personality – as a musician and as Lynn Harrell. I wasn't aware of the judges, I just knew that I was making music. And I loved every second that I was free of Self 1.'

Choosing alternative strategies

How do you choose between the many different strategies that we've been discussing? The best guide is your own experience, of course, and I'd encourage you to experiment and discover what works best for you. In case you don't know quite where to begin, you may want to start with one of the techniques suggested below.

If you notice you are paralysed with fear about the *consequences* of your performance, you might experiment with reassessing your *goals*. What does your music mean to you? What are your experience goals? What are your performance goals? When you have reconnected with your goals, go out there and play.

If you notice you are having a problem concentrating on the music because of the *instruction* and *criticism* of your Self 1 voice, you may find it helpful to choose AWARENESS techniques. Focus on sights, sounds, feelings and understanding. These techniques will help you to switch your attention back to the music.

If *doubt* and *fear* are the sources of your problem, you might explore *trust* techniques to allow Self 2 to perform. Choose one of the techniques for letting go, and trust that Self 2 will usually perform better than Self 1. It can be scary to relinquish that tenuous sense of control, but Self 2 possesses a marvellous reservoir of confidence and skill.

Dealing with External Interference

We overcome obstacles such as self-doubt, anxiety and fear of failure in the inner arena. But there are also times when external factors beyond our control interfere with our playing. They're the moments that make for great stories after the concert, but they're not so easy to handle at the time. Have you ever tried to play while your partner is chewing gum? Cinnamon-flavoured gum, at that?

A broken string, a baby crying in the audience, or a stomach ache can all throw you off balance. You could be playing in an ensemble where your microphone blocks your view of the conductor. You may need to stand in without rehearsal for a colleague who has the flu. You have to cope. What to do? What are your choices?

In circumstances like these, you can freeze in your tracks, do nothing – and fail; you can perform in a tense and distracted way – and fail; or you can sprinkle a little Inner Game into the situation. Not too surprisingly, this last option is the approach that I'd recommend. It's the strategy for success.

Here are four options open to the Inner Game player who needs to cope with an external emergency:

1. You can accept the obstacle without stopping your activity.

2. You can ignore the obstacle and use awareness techniques to refocus your attention on your playing.

3. You can alter the situation by physically changing some aspect of the obstacle.

4. You can make the obstacle work for you.

Accept the interference

We have seen that one way to deal with internal interference – nerves before a concert, say – is to remain aware of it, to 'allow' it rather than to fight it. Elizabeth, who felt jittery before a cello concert, discovered that by accepting her nerves, she could play as if she was 'coming down a ski slope feeling really exhilarated'. She realized that she enjoyed feeling the adrenaline coursing through her. An excitement that could easily have turned into panic if she'd fought it allowed her to speed up her reflexes and enjoy her playing even more when she chose to accept it.

The same principle can be used in dealing with external interference. Suppose there's a heating system in your practice room that keeps turning on and shutting off with loud groans in the pipes. Or a baby crying. Or the neighbours are playing the radio. If you can still hear your playing above the sound of these infuriating and distracting noises, you have a choice. You can become infuriated and distracted, or you can 'allow' the sounds to be there.

An interruption only becomes an interruption when we perceive it as such. Once you realize that your music and these extraneous noises can coexist, the noises are less likely to siphon your attention away from the music. One way to handle this kind of distraction is to accept, acknowledge and allow it – and bring your focus back to the music.

Use awareness techniques to refocus attention

When I first realized that I could switch my attention to anything I chose as easily as I switch channels on my TV, I was frankly amazed. We often feel as if an interruption demands our attention, as if there's nothing we can do about distractions but be distracted. But we can choose not to stay on that wavelength.

If a physician's paging bleeper goes off in the softest passage of a Beethoven piano concerto, it's not as if the bleeper is likely to keep on bleeping for the next two movements, but the spell that the pianist has been weaving in the audience is likely to be broken.

What does John Browning do about it if he's playing the concerto with the New York Philharmonic? He has phenomental concentration, and he's entirely swept up in the music. He continues to play without hesitation. The audience senses his focus, the distraction is quickly forgotten, and the music continues.

Exercise: Inviting distractions

I'd like to suggest an exercise that can help you to achieve this kind of concentration when you're performing by shortening the 'recovery time' after a momentary interruption. It's helpful to cultivate the attitude that momentary interruptions are normal and to be expected. This allows you to be confident in your ability to continue playing after a sudden interruption – or after a momentary slip on your own part.

1. Ask a friend to work with you as your 'distractor'. Supply your friend with the 'distractor's toolkit' – an alarm clock, a radio and a hair dryer.

2. Now ask your friend to sit behind you and mimic a Self 1 conversation while you play a piece of your choice. Have him set the alarm, switch the radio on and off unexpectedly, and use the hair dryer from time to time.

3. Don't worry if you're distracted: that's part of the purpose of the exercise. Your job is simply to be aware of how long it takes you to recover from an interruption and refocus on the music.

4. Repeat the exercise and notice the changes in your recovery time.

When I first introduced this exercise to my conservatory students, it seemed to be a unique and somewhat radical technique. But I have since learned from the Suzuki piano teacher Peggie Luey that she often 'plays distraction' with her young students.

Once you are used to dealing with disruptions and distractions, and have come to expect and even welcome them, much of their power to disturb you vanishes. This exercise can help you to shorten your recovery time.

Do something about it

Many of the obstacles to successful performance can be dealt with by taking some simple action to deal with them, but in the slightly panicked state that can precede any important event, we often forget to notice what can be done.

If you mouth is dry with the anticipation you feel before a

musical entrance, you can take a sip of water, or increase your saliva flow by gently biting your tongue. Taking a sip of water makes a lot more sense than increasing your level of worry and getting distracted from the music.

If you notice your heartbeat is increasing and your breath is becoming shallow before a solo, you can gently slow down your breathing by becoming aware of it, and as your breathing deepens, your heart rate will decrease.

Examine the obstacles to your playing and see whether there are any simple, physical changes you can make that will deal with them. I have known keyboard players who used spray deodorant on their fingertips to prevent sweaty hands. Some players use mild lubricants on their guitars to prevent them from becoming sticky.

Quickly surveying your alternatives can sometimes produce surprising results in even seemingly hopeless situations. I remember the day last summer when I was stopped in a traffic snarl a mile and a half away from a concert in the park, fifteen minutes before the performance was due to begin. There was no sign that the traffic was likely to start moving again, and I felt like panicking.

The first signs of panic now seem like warning signals to me (in fact, that's probably an important Inner Game technique in itself). I realized that I was dealing with an 'external obstacle' and began to run through my options in my head.

1. I could accept the traffic jam and wait for it to clear.
2. I could ignore the traffic and listen to the radio.
3. I could take some physical action to deal with the situation. I considered honking my horn, but it wouldn't have made much difference, and anyway I play bass, not horn . . . I could tear my hair . . . I could tell a policeman I was in the orchestra, but he wouldn't have been able to do much about it . . . Or, wait a minute . . . I realized that I can run a mile in under eight minutes and could probably manage a mile and a half in twelve.

I took an extremely physical action to deal with the obstacle. I pulled my car to the side of the road and ran like the wind, slipping into my seat at the concert with a couple of minutes to spare.

Make the interference work for you

There are times when you can't accept or change your circumstances and your only choice may be to find ways to make the interference work for you. Sometimes this means simply accepting that the situation won't allow you to achieve your primary goal and finding other goals that you can accomplish instead. If I'd had to carry my double bass to the park for that concert, I'd never have made it in time.

Perhaps I'd have realized I would simply have to wait for the traffic to clear and would miss the first piece. I could have decided to listen to some music in the car or perform isometric exercises on the steering wheel. These alternative goals would at least have given me an alternative to sitting there feeling thoroughly frustrated.

There are also times when you can't avoid the interference, but can choose to use it to the advantage of your primary goals. If a colleague is practising loudly in the next room and you are unable simply to accept the distraction or ignore it, and if you've looked for ways to change the situation – but there aren't any other practice rooms available – you need to make your obstacle work for you, not against you.

Perhaps this means listening to your friend's playing and seeing what you can learn from it. Or playing a duet with him (with or without his knowing). Perhaps you will want to play a piece in a contrasting style or to play a different piece at the same tempo.

Peggy asked me what she could do about a cold sore in her mouth that was making it very painful for her to play her horn. We checked first to see if there was any way she could play without the sore hurting, but it simply couldn't be done. She needed to take at least one day's break from her practising.

Peggy made good use of the time that had suddenly opened up in her busy schedule. Not only did she find a medication that cleared up the problem; she also took the opportunity to hunt up and listen to a recording of her favourite horn player performing the same piece, worked on her fingerings and phrasing 'away from the instrument', and took the time to find a new piece she wanted to start learning.

The key to coping with external obstacles in every case is to expand your frame of reference to include things that you have little or no control over. By accepting inevitable distractions and obstacles when they occur, you can use your creativity to find your own variants on these four approaches.

9 Improving the quality of musical experience

I recently played the bass part in a rehearsal of Verdi's opera *Rigoletto*. My part was small and boring: a short note on the first and third beats of each bar – boom, rest, boom, rest, boom, rest, over and over again. Occasionally, the first note would change pitch, and once in a while I had the pleasure and excitement of holding a note longer. 'Thirty-two bars of this same stuff, and then I get to change notes,' I told myself. 'This gets old fast – I could probably turn on a tape of my bass part, and no one would be any the wiser.'

I knew I couldn't really slip away from the rehearsal, though, and wanted to create a more challenging and satisfying experience than I'd been having so far. I hated the part so much I wished I could make it disappear – so I decided not to look at a single note while I was playing.

I memorized the music several bars at a time and found to my amazement that as soon as I stopped looking at the music I began listening more closely. The opera came to life for me. I heard the voices on stage and even listened to my own playing with a new awareness. I began to put more expression into that simple pattern of notes – and my boredom went away.

Heightening your experience while performing

One thing led to another, and I began to apply this same technique when I was playing more complex music. I would keep my eyes a few notes ahead of where I was playing so I could focus more on the sound and meaning of the music. Playing became more of a challenge for me, and my performance improved musically. I found I was playing more of the maybe ninety per cent of the music that's not written in the score.

I consider my time to be valuable – to me. I'm willing just to 'write off' hours at a stretch as tedious or boring. I don't enjoy being bored. I'm not volunteering for it if I can avoid it. And as I found out when I played that simple bass line in *Rigoletto*, I can avoid boredom. Boredom is what I feel when I don't feel sufficiently challenged by what I'm doing. But I can always choose to find challenge in what would otherwise seem boring circumstances.

In many ways, the opposite of boredom is feeling there's too much challenge. But there's often only a fine line between feeling a little scared by the challenge you're facing and feeling exhilarated by it. Just as you can usually avoid boredom by adding challenge, you can usually turn a scary moment into a time of discovery by stepping back and taking one thing at a time – Tim Gallwey's doctrine of the easy – or by letting go to that part of you that really knows how to do it.

We will probably still feel some uncertainty accompanying the actual process of letting go; however, this heightening of our nervous system's alertness can be put to good use. As we begin to feel the power of the music beginning to sweep over us, this alertness prepares the body to play.

If you're playing one of Brahms' magnificent symphonies, for example, you may find that your conscious thinking has stopped. Something in the music moves your hand at the moment of your entrance. Your nervousness turns into exhilaration as your body responds, and you are caught up in the power and momentum of the music.

One major element in 'letting go' is our vulnerability. Much of the excitement in playing live music comes from not knowing what will happen in each performance.

If you see a film for a second or third time, you may be able to follow some aspects of the plot in more detail, and notice the cinematography and the quality of the acting, but the film is unlikely to have as much overall impact as it did the first time you saw it – because you already 'know the outcome' of the story. But even though the notes of a piece of music are familiar, we never know how we're going to perform.

The vulnerability we feel when we know that every new performance brings new opportunities for disaster or triumph, and the vulnerability we feel when we let go to Self 2's control, are what keep us on our toes – and bring the experience of music making alive.

In order to stay (or become) vulnerable, we first have to accept the possibility of failure. Itzhak Perlman appears to play effortlessly, with endless virtuosity. He executes difficult passages with the flair of a tightrope walker, and his audience can sense just how close to the impossible he comes. While he rarely falters in his playing, the excitement he projects comes from his reckless courage in the face of potential disaster.

Self 1 is concerned about the possibility of failure, but unless we become vulnerable and accept that possibility, we can never know how far Self 2 can take us. Most people are amazed by their own natural abilities and feel humbled when they explore and experience Self 2's understanding of the music.

When the music really comes alive, it means the performers have put themselves at risk, and to risk an interpretation, to risk exposing yourself to the music, means confronting the risk of failure. We need to accept the possibility of failure, stay in the moment, trust Self 2's ability to play beyond what Self 1 is capable of, and give the music everything we've got.

Heightening your experience while practising

When we are analysing, learning and practising a piece, our feelings don't necessarily have to be linked to the feelings expressed in the music the way they do when we're actually performing.

Practising often seems boring or excessively disciplined and dull. But it's quite possible to enjoy your practice time and still programme those muscles. You can learn by watching a master perform in a movie or live demonstration. In fact, our most effective learning may take place when we are having a great time – and almost completely unaware that we are 'learning' anything.

I once asked my students to practise for an hour while having just as much fun as they could devise. They got up to all sorts of strange tricks, as you can imagine. Two oboe students exchanged their unique, custom-adjusted instruments and played duets together. A horn player practised while walking among the trees. A clarinetist decided to play his music in a jazz style, improvising on every phrase. A pianist practised while standing up. A cellist reversed his hands, and played left-handed for the first time. Another student improvised scales while listening to a baseball game, pacing his playing against the energy of the game the way cinema organists in the early days used to play along with the film: when the game was slow, so were his scales, and he burst into a flurry of activity when the game got hot.

Every one of my students learned and accomplished much more than they normally did in an hour of practice. The oboists found they played almost as well on strange instruments, and sometimes better. The horn player's music gained a new openness and sense of freedom from his practice outside. The clarinetist discovered she was able to improvise much more inventively than she had given herself credit for, and her classical playing gained in flexibility as a result. When the cellist played left handed, he noticed he was paying much more attention to the resistance of the string than he usually did. With the heightened awareness that playing left handed gave him, his tone improved when he went back to playing with his right hand. And the student who had accompanied the baseball game realized that his scales could be played in many different ways: they didn't always have to sound boring. And he noticed he also learned more about his instrument when he varied the style and dynamics of his scales.

This experiment taught us two things:

1. That if you have fun while you practise, you may also learn more and perform better.

2. That you don't have to be serious and tense in order to learn.

You don't have to be analytical to arrive at the best fingering solutions. You don't have to suffer pain in order to execute a quick motion. You don't have to gasp for breath in order to have sufficient air. And you don't have to be a nervous wreck before a performance in order to play well.

Exercise: Having fun while you practise

1. Practise for an hour, making a goal of having fun while you do it. You might choose one of the approaches my students used, or perhaps decide to

> watch TV while practising your exercises;
> alter your instrument by putting paper between the strings;
> play without a valve or finger;
> change the tuning of your instrument;
> record yourself on tape and play a duet with yourself;
> sing and play simultaneously;
> play your music backwards;
> invent a musical game of your own.

2. After your hour of experiment, make a list of all the things you learned about your instrument, your self, your attention and the music.

3. Notice what you learned that can be of value in a more conventional practice session, and spend a few minutes of your regular practice time repeating or further exploring this kind of fun experience.

You may find you want to change the goals you set yourself when you practise to allow more of your enthusiasm and enjoyment to be present. When practice is a delight to which you can look forward, as well as a discipline that helps you master your craft, you're well on the road to fine musicianship.

Expanding your understanding of stress

Another way for you to alter your feeling about 'boring' practice is to begin to focus on musical stress, or dissonance. Most people perceive tension and stress as something to avoid, but it's an important part of creating an artistic experience.

Most Western music is based on a harmonic system of creating and resolving dissonance. Effectively, this means that the music gains much of its power from setting up musical tensions and stresses, and then resolving them. Mahler's superb crafting of movements full of chaos, warlike sonorities and dramatic dissonances is essential to build the tension that he ultimately resolves in his serene and harmonious endings. This creation and resolution of tension is what brings the performer and listener a real feeling of beauty and satisfaction in the music.

It's not as though music is alone in this, either. A gripping movie, play or novel is one that builds tension and suspense – and then releases it. This is one of those places where the arts can teach us about life, for life, too, contains its times of discord and tension, and its moments of relaxation and repose.

When we realize that what at first looks like a stressful or negative experience can be understood as a 'dissonance' that can lead to resolution, we can begin to accept the stressful moments and flow with them instead of resisting them. The times that we look back on with the greatest pleasure are often those when we experienced a full measure of obstacles and stresses and were able to bring them to a harmonious resolution. Our goal is to be able to 'experience our experience' fully, without classifying it as either bad or good.

Solving a musical problem means facing the problem and finding a resolution to it. It's another example of the way in which seeming dissonance leads to harmony and growth. As psychiatrist M. Scott Peck observed in his book *The Road Less Travelled*, 'It is in this whole process of meeting and solving problems that life has its meaning . . . Problems call forth our courage and our wisdom; indeed they create our courage and our wisdom. It is only because of problems that we grow . . . It is for this reason that wise people learn not to dread but actually welcome problems.'

Here again, the secret is to value all your feelings and all your experiences – the down times along with the up, the rough with the smooth. It's your life that's made up of all those moments, and the more you allow yourself actually to feel and experience, the more alive you'll be. And that sense of aliveness will translate directly into lively, deeply felt music.

Valuing the way you feel – as well as your accomplishments

Exercise: Some memorable accomplishments

Make a list of some of the times when you have had a wonderful and memorable experience connected with your music and felt a real sense of accomplishment. Perhaps you'll remember the sense of achievement you felt when you graduated from college, the thrill of your first public performance, the day you were accepted into an orchestra, band or choir, or even the excitement you felt when you purchased your first fine quality instrument after months of skimping and saving.

Now ask yourself how much of your pride and delight on each of these occasions came from what you accomplished, how much was a matter of the feelings that went into your accomplishment, and how much was the result of what you learned as you were getting there.

How much would you have valued the experience if it had been handed to you on a plate? If you'd never attended college and the degree had been awarded you by a computer malfunction? If you were a multi-millionaire and suspected you might have been given your orchestral seat in the hope that you'd donate a sizeable sum to the orchestra? If your parents owned a musical instrument store and you could have any instrument you liked just by asking for it?

Wouldn't some of your most memorable accomplishments seem less memorable, perhaps even meaningless, if you'd simply been able to click your fingers and a genie in a bottle had done the rest? Isn't the whole experience – everything you felt and did that led up to your accomplishment – at least as valuable to you as the accomplishment itself?

Our most worthwhile and memorable accomplishments usually result from our enthusiasm and our dreams. But they also are likely to have involved many hours, months or years of dedicated work, uncertainty and sacrifice. Certainly, there was plenty of stress and tension, but as in a fine piece of music, the tensions were finally resolved.

There are days when we wake up in the morning and the world looks full of promise and excitement, and other days when everything appears drab and uninteresting. In the final analysis it is our state of consciousness, the way we look at the world, that determines the kind of experience we have.

This chapter has been concerned with the times when you feel there's not enough challenge and the times when you feel there's altogether too much. Both of these attitudes have a certain validity, but in each case a small shift in your attitude can allow a painful and difficult task to become interesting and exciting.

So much depends on the degree to which you value the moments, the minutes and hours, of your life. If your life is precious to you, you will want your practice time to be both enjoyable and musically rewarding. And you will want to see the 'musical' pattern behind times of difficulty and stress, so you can move on through them and reach the resolution.

What is it that makes a musical experience come alive for you? Why should you value the experience you are having? Why do you spend so much time making music in the first place? What is it about music? How can it be so incredibly beautiful?

If you occasionally pause and reassess the experience you are actually having while you practise or perform, you may find it affects some of the daily choices you make about practice and performance. It may refresh your enthusiasm, heighten your ability to learn, and put you more deeply in touch with the music than before.

10 Teaching and learning

I'm not much good at throwing a Frisbee. So when my two sons, Zach and Adam, asked me to show them how to do it, I tried – with very little success. I showed them where each finger should be placed on the Frisbee and how to follow through with the body after you've thrown the disc. But my throws weren't very proficient. Adam quickly lost interest, but Zach was eager to learn.

I tried to describe the whole sequence of events in words, but translating a very quick but graceful motion into a series of step-by-step instructions proved difficult, too. Zach began to pry me with questions. 'What happens if I curl my fingers under the rim, Dad? Will I throw it better? Which finger did you say went on top? Should it go like this? How will I ever remember this position? I feel like my hand is glued to the Frisbee. How am I going to let go of it?'

Zach finally did let go of the Frisbee, and it went right into the ground. He was frustrated and disappointed that he couldn't make the Frisbee fly, and he, too, lost interest.

The next day I took the kids to see *Tron*, a movie in which the hero uses a Frisbee-like weapon to fight the bad guys. He whirls his Frisbee with incredible accuracy, and the disc demolishes everything in its path. The boys' eyes never left the screen. They were completely absorbed in the hero's battle against the forces of evil – and his incredible Frisbee technique.

Our $2.50 bucket of popcorn had entitled us to an official Tron Frisbee, and as soon as Zach and Adam were out in the parking lot, they began to throw it. I watched them in amazement. They were throwing the Frisbee with perfect form fifty yards or more.

I'd been trying to teach them for months, if the truth be known. And yet once they'd seen an effective hand grip, watched the relationship of the body to the throwing arm, and absorbed some of the hero's confidence, they quickly 'became' the hero, complete with his Frisbee technique. They had learned in a couple of hours what I had spent months trying to teach them – by experiencing the way it should be done, as demonstrated by a master. And I had relearned an important lesson for a teacher: that detailed verbal instructions are seldom as effective as experience.

This kind of teaching is quite different from the 'do this' style of instruction with which everything from tennis to music is usually taught. Instead of the teacher telling a student to 'change the tempo in the last bar,' for example, they are more likely to ask questions that focus the student's attention on the problem areas. This allows the student to make the necessary corrections without being told exactly what to do.

This approach to teaching and learning de-emphasizes 'instruction' and relies more on the body's ability to sense problems and change them without first translating them into words. It's an approach that encourages students to be their own teachers. And it includes the kind of effortless learning by which Adam and Zach picked up the art of throwing the Frisbee.

Watching someone else is one of the ways to learn. But learning can involve more than just visual learning. It also makes use of hearing, touch and the emotions. In each case, however, the emphasis is on learning by some form of experience, rather than learning by following instructions.

Letting the body teach the body

My first bass lesson was very frustrating. I had never heard a bass solo in my life, and my eighty-year-old teacher asked me to play one. Then he told me it was no good. He explained that I needed to straighten my left arm, although I hadn't the faintest idea why. He told me I was using the wrong fingering, though I had very little idea what the finger-ings were for. And he told me I had played out of tune, though he didn't tell me where in the piece I'd done it. Then he suggested I should practise harder so I would do better next week.

Some time after this, I heard Gary Karr play a concert. Like his father, his grandfather, and his great-grandfather before him, he was a virtuoso bass player. He was only a few years older than I was, and yet he was already an international celebrity. As you can imagine, I watched and listened to his performance very closely. He even played some of the pieces I was studying in my lessons.

What I learned from that concert was worth ten years of lessons. I saw how effortlessly Gary Karr played, I felt the meaning and power of the music, the sound went into my heart and soul, and I got my first glimpse of what it must be like when the player's body 'merges' with his instrument.

It was a turning point for me. When the time came for my next lesson, I found that by slowing my bow speed and using my body weight rather than finger pressure, I was able to produce a fuller sound. I imitated Gary Karr's wider and slower vibrato, which added some majesty to my sound. I imagined how Karr would play, and instead of hurrying through to the end, I gave each passage time to breathe.

I found I could 'translate' my experience of watching and listening to Gary Karr into my own playing.

I feel there's something almost unfair about trying to teach a skill by putting it into words. We learn so much more when we learn through our senses and our experience. Maybe there are 'information' subjects where verbal instruction works best, but music is something the body is going to have to perform and it's best learned by the body that's going to do the performing.

Professor Leighton Conkling of Ohio University told me he was teaching a class in bass. In fact, he noticed that he was far more successful as a bass teacher than he was when he taught his own instrument, the cello. He told me he knew too much about the cello and that his knowledge often got in the way when he was coaching his students. 'I think I sometimes confuse them with my good suggestions,' he told me.

Since he doesn't know all the answers on the bass, he explores the instrument with his students and lets them discover what works best for themselves. Instead of marking the bowings, the fingerings and the phrasing and telling them exactly how he wants them to play, he invites them to experiment with a variety of different fingerings. His students sometimes play a piece with three or four different bowings and then decide with him which one allows the music to come through most clearly. He also encourages his bass students to listen to different recordings of the pieces they're learning, so that their understanding and feel for the music comes from more than one source, one teacher.

Professor Conkling's bass students learn more this way than his cello students do when he 'gives them the right answers'. And his ultimate dream, he told me, would be 'to find a way to communicate everything I know about the cello by means of a process of discovery – not by instruction.'

The problem with 'do this' instructions

Instructions that tell a student to 'do this' run into problems. They ask the student to achieve certain results which the student may not feel he or she can produce: ' Hold the bass with your left hand two inches from the top of the neck, with your thumb curved, your first finger one and a half inches across from and behind the thumb, the second finger opposite the thumb, and the third and fourth fingers an inch and a half apart. Don't be stiff.'

There are various ways in which a student can feel unable to translate this kind of verbal command into a physical action.

1. Students may not understand what's required. 'How far is an inch and a half? And what do you mean by curving the thumb?'

2. They may understand the instruction but have a hard time creating the desired effect with their bodies. 'I can't seem to get my fingers an inch and a half apart.' They may also experience some degree of self-doubt when their bodies don't seem able to conform to what their teachers expect of them.

3. They may understand the instruction, but the task may simply be beyond their physical capability. 'My fingers don't reach an inch and a half. They're too short.'
4. Sometimes the instructions aren't even accurate, or contradict the student's experience. 'This doesn't look right to me, and it isn't the way Mr Grodner holds his hand.'
5. The instructions may be fine, the students may understand them and be physically capable of carrying them out, but when too many of them are piled one on top of each other, it may be more than the mind can handle. 'I'm so confused – where does the third finger go?'
6. Students sometimes even manage to follow all the instructions, only to find they have forgotten them the next day.
7. Finally, there are times when students simply don't agree with the instructions they receive, and part of their attention is diverted into finding other ways to get around the problem. While this may lead to some fruitful experiential learning, it certainly gets in the way of learning from the instructions.

Instructions that include the words 'try to . . .' are also liable to cause problems. As we saw in Chapter 3, the suggestion of 'trying' creates doubt in our ability to succeed. We don't talk about 'trying' to sit down on a chair; we know we can do it, and we do.

'Try' instructions tend to cause anxiety, and then we are liable to tense up and 'try too hard', making us fail at tasks we might otherwise accomplish without any problems. Like 'do this' instructions, 'try' instructions sometimes cause the problems they're intended to avoid.

The advantages of awareness instructions

Awareness instructions put students into an entirely different frame of mind. They are based on the students' own experience – their ability to learn by noticing what's happening. They don't involve 'right' or 'wrong' ways to go about things. They don't involve a complex series of steps that are easily confused or forgotten. They never demand more of the body than it is capable of handling. They don't invoke doubt. And as a result, they free students from doubt, confusion, frustration and discouragement.

The ironic thing is that almost all 'do this' and 'try' instructions could be rephrased as awareness instructions. Those incredibly complex and frustrating instructions for holding the bass fiddle in your left hand would be simple to turn into an awareness instruction: 'Notice how evenly each of your fingertips transfers the weight from your arm. Notice the most comfortable place for your thumb, somewhere opposite your first and second fingers.'

With awareness instructions like this, there's no demand that students remember how far apart the fingers are to be placed; they can tell when they've found the correct position by the feeling of weight on their fingertips. The second part of the instruction doesn't imply that there's any right or wrong position for the thumb. Whatever feels comfortable to the individual is correct.

These instructions don't have to be memorized: once the body has felt its way into the correct position, it will be able to return to it. The body learns because it is free to focus on what feels good and works best.

Awareness exercises only ask one thing of the conscious mind: that it should *pay attention* to what's happening, not to what's right or wrong, good or bad. The key is simply to be aware of what is going on. That's the way we all learned to walk, and that's the way we learn best. Verbal 'do' instructions just can't compare with this kind of body learning. Music teachers have little difficulty teaching students who speak a different language, and the reason isn't far to find: when we minimize the use of verbal instructions, we also cut down on Self 1 interference.

How to change 'do this' instructions into awareness instructions

The biggest challenge in coaching teachers in the techniques of the Inner Game is to help them find the right words to create an experience for their students. It can be difficult for a coach or teacher to change longstanding teaching habits, even when they recognize the drawbacks of 'do this' instructions.

I've found that the key is to use certain phrases that unlock useful responses from students. Here are some phrases that you can begin to listen for that signal a 'do this' instruction coming up:

> Do such and such.
> This is difficult, but . . .
> Play it this way.
> Make it better.
> Please try harder.
> Now relax.
> Let's get it right this time.

Use the Inner Game to deal with these instructions – just become aware of them when you use them, without blaming or criticizing yourself, and they'll begin to drop away on their own.

Here are some other phrases that emphasize the students' own awareness and experience, which you can gradually introduce in place of the 'do this' phrases listed above:

> Be aware of . . .
> Listen for . . .
> How does it feel when you . . .
> Tell me the difference you notice between . . .
> What do you hear when you . . .
> Pay attention to the . . .
> Let's see if . . .
> Notice the feeling you get when . . .

The way to change a 'do this' instruction into an awareness instruction is simply to rephrase it so that the focus of attention is on the student's experience. Here are some examples. I've included possible student reactions to the 'do this' instructions in parentheses.

'Do this' instruction:	Awareness instruction:
Draw the bow perpendicular to the bow string. (I'll try hard to keep it straight.)	Notice the angle of the bow when the resistance is steady.

'Do this' instruction:	Awareness instruction:
Don't clip your consonants at the ends of the phrases. (Which phrases? How should I pronounce them? Why?)	Listen to the sound of the consonants at the ends of your phrases. See if you can clearly hear the words.
Play louder as you go to the higher notes. (How much louder? Which notes are wrong? Am I loud enough now?)	Pay attention to the degree of increase in volume as you play higher notes.
You must play these bars forte, and you're too loud. (How loud should I be? It could be the pianist's fault.)	Notice what forte level allows the piano still to be heard.
Play the piano with your fingers curved at a 90-degree angle from the third knuckle. (Which is the third knuckle? Can it be at 95-degrees? What about the fourth finger?)	Notice the difference in the way the support of your arm feels when your fingers are slightly curved, and when they are more curved. Play in whatever way lets your fingers feel the most support.
Play with the correct intonation. (What's wrong with my pitch? Am I too high, or too low?)	Be aware of your intonation. Notice when or if you're playing sharp or flat. Notice how sharp or how flat.

It takes patience and imagination to learn to rephrase 'do this' instructions into awareness instructions on an ongoing basis, and I encourage you to experiment for yourself and find your own way of phrasing things so that you bring out the best in your students.

Sometimes you may feel it would be quicker and more effective simply to tell someone 'do this' instead of asking them whether they can tell what's missing. You'll usually find you can still give a specific suggestion, while rephrasing it in awareness terms. For instance, you might say something like 'Let's run an experiment: use the fourth finger this time, and see if it works better on the shift than the second.'

I've found that as a teacher I'm in a somewhat curious position. On the one hand, I like to feel I'm in charge of things (that little voice that likes to be in control again), and I like to be able to take credit for knowing the answers to problems and to feel essential to my student's process. On the other hand, my deepest goal in teaching is to help my students learn to the best of their ability, and that means avoiding mental obstacles.

When I measure my success as a teacher by how much my students actually learn, I find that awareness instructions are the most powerful.

The following instructions may help you to explore teaching (and learning) using the awareness approach. They ask the player to be aware of something (usually in the realms of sight, sound, physical or emotional feeling, or understanding) in relationship to a goal which is clearly stated. For example, if your goal is to stay in tune, the awareness instruction would tell you to 'notice whether you're sharp or flat on the C natural.'

I have listed the instructions according to the various groups of instruments, but many of them could also be applied to instruments in other groups. And in each case I've included the equivalent 'do this' instructions in parentheses.

Visual Awareness Instructions

Strings

Notice the vertical pattern of the tip of your bow during the even notes. (Keep the bow stroke even.)

Look to see where your bow is when your sound seems to be thin. (Keep your bow close to the bridge.)

Notice the position of your elbow when the shift sounds correct. (Keep your elbow down when shifting.)

Notice the angle of your thumb when the fingers of your right hand feel most flexible. (Keep the thumb curved.)

Wind

Notice which fingers aren't completely covering the pads when the pitch doesn't speak. (Keep your fingers on the pads.)

See if you're still playing when there's a rest in the music. (Don't play during the rests.)

Keyboard

Notice what sort of curvature of your fingers lets you play with the least effort and best support. (Play with your fingers curved.)

Imagine there's a ruler balancing on your wrists as you play. (Don't flop your wrists.)

See how close your fingers are to the keys when your semiquavers sound correct. (Keep your fingers close to the keys.)

Voice

Take a look at your body posture when you feel the maximum resonance. (Stand erect when you sing).

See if your face reflects the meaning of the music. (Look more expressive while you sing.)

Auditory Awareness Instructions

Strings

Notice how the character of your sound relates to the meaning of the music. (Play with more tonal character.)

Listen to find out whether your vibrato is changing during the more important notes in this phrase. (Use more vibrato in your phrasing.)

Can you hear any changes in your sound quality as you play louder? (Don't scratch when you get louder.)

Wind

Check how the tension in the muscles below your lip is affecting your sound quality. (Keep your chin flat and firm.)

Move your jaw in and out until you get the kind of sound you want. (Keep your jaw in the correct place.)

Notice how the lip support around your mouthpiece feels when you're producing a sustained sound. (Keep your lips firm.)

Listen to the rhythmic clicking of the keys, and see if they reflect the rhythm of the notes. (Play with a more precise tempo.)

Keyboard

Listen for any differences in the sounds of attacks that are marked similarly. (Play more evenly.)

Sing the notes in your head as you play, and notice where there are differences between your singing and your playing. (Make it more melodic.)

Notice if you can detect a difference between the sound of your thumb and the fingers. (Don't accent the thumb.)

Voice

Notice whether your pitch is sharp or flat on the high D natural. (Sing the high D in tune.)

Notice whether the volume of each note is getting louder as you go higher. (Get the crescendo right.)

When the sound seems to be thin, notice the support you're getting from your lower abdominal muscles. (Maintain proper breath support.)

Feeling Awareness Instructions

Strings

Feel the flexibility in your arm when you play the faster notes. (Don't stiffen up in the fast passages.)

Maintain an even arm weight on the bow as you play each note. (Keep your elbow up.)

Notice which parts of your body are moving with the pulse of the music. (Conduct with your body.)

Check whether your body is feeling the emotions that the music is expressing. (Get more involved in your playing.)

Wind

Notice whether your neck muscles are stiff when the music gets more difficult. (Relax your neck.)

Feel which finger pads are not down on the keys when the notes don't speak. (Keep the pads down on the keys.)

Pay attention to any movement in your lower back when you take a good breath. (Breathe lower down.)

Keyboard

Do you feel a difference in tension between your left and right shoulders as you play? (Relax your right shoulder.)

Notice how the steady pulse feels during the melodic passage. (Don't rush the melody.)

How does your back feel when you lean over the keyboard? (Sit up straighter.)

Notice how much weight is on your fingertips during the loud passages. (Keep the weight on the fingertips.)

Voice

Notice how your throat feels when you move to the higher register. (Relax the neck muscles in the high register.)

Notice the change in sound when your throat feels closed. (Keep the throat open.)

Find the best body position for easy breathing. (Sit up straight.)

Notice if the abdominal area expands as you inhale. (Breathe from the diaphragm.)

Understanding Awareness Instructions

Understanding awareness exercises are usually much more closely tied in to the meaning of a particular piece than the other, more directly sensory exercises. I have included a couple of examples here to give you the general idea; this is another place where creativity and sensitivity to the particular situation are needed.

Strings

Does the off-the-string or the on-the-string bowing sound more Baroque? (Play the passage on the string.)

Voice

Notice when your tone quality best reflects the meaning of the text. (This is meant to be a very moving passage. Give it a better quality of sound.)

Making the switch

There's usually a period of adjustment in the relationship between teacher and student when the teacher switches over and begins to use awareness instructions. This may feel awkward at times. The teacher may feel uncertain of how things are going to turn out at first, and may not feel comfortable releasing too much control. And the student may feel a little adrift and uncertain in the absence of specific instructions: students don't always feel comfortable trusting their Self 2 potential, and sometimes feel uneasy when they are asked to ignore Self 1's advice in favour of Self 2.

This can be particularly true of students who are studying under distinguished teachers. Such people often have a strong tendency to follow instructions without taking responsibility for the results. Even when the instructions don't seem to work, the students may ignore what sounds right or feels best because they have previously been told to play a certain way. When new problems arise, these students often have to return to their professor for answers, clarifications and further instructions.

The problem here is that a sense of dependency arises in the relationship between teacher and student, and when these students need to 'go it alone' in the world outside, they may find it a difficult adjustment to make. They haven't been taught to solve problems for themselves, to listen to the music they are making, or to draw on other sources for additional understanding. An important learning shift takes place when these students learn how to pay attention to their own Inner Game teacher within them.

Some students, however, are simply not comfortable making their own discoveries. Inner Game coaches need to be sensitive to these issues and use their best judgement in creating a balanced student-teacher relationship. Some students respond best to direct, authoritative guidance and want to be shown specific ways to deal with musical problems. Others will be delighted to be in charge of their own discovery process and will rarely want to be told what to do.

I always regard it as a positive sign when my students tell me that they are progressing well with their immediate musical goals but feel I am 'withholding something' from them. This tells me that I'm managing to get across what I know by guiding them to their own experience of it – while they are still waiting for the instruction that tells them what to do.

Isaac Stern did a magical job of communicating without words or specific 'do this' instructions during his tour of China, which was recorded in the wonderful film *From Mao to Mozart*. He managed to accomplish a great deal of musical instruction through the use of gestures and mimicry, with a minimum of discussion. He was able to transcend language, cultural and personal barriers – using only his violin, his tone of voice and a very few words.

11 The Inner Game listener

The Seattle Symphony Orchestra are giving their fourth concert in a series. The programme includes works by Beethoven, Mozart and Richard Strauss. You arrive just in time for the first piece, Beethoven's *Coriolanus* Overture. The music begins, but you are not quite ready to listen yet. 'Looks like the conductor forgot to comb his hair – or maybe it's a new fashion,' you think. 'Let's see, did I leave the keys in the car? I wish the people in the row behind us would stop talking. I'm not really in the mood for Beethoven; when are they going to get to the Mozart? I wonder if we'll run into Jim at the interval.'

Listening to music seems as if it should be the simplest thing in the world, but it often isn't. It can seem difficulty because we don't understand the 'language' the music is speaking; because we are 'listening in the wrong place', trying to find feelings 'outside us' in the music when they have been inside us all along; because we bring expectations with us that aren't satisfied; or simply because we're distracted by the people around us.

For one or more of these reasons, many of us find ourselves preoccupied with Self 1 conversations at the start of a concert, knowing only too well that they keep us from becoming really absorbed in the music. Outside distractions, such as a child chewing gum in the row in front of you, can be bad enough. And when the music is particularly difficult to understand, or when we just think it is, our distractions and worries can become even more of a problem.

If we want to silence those sabotaging inner conversations and worries, there are three things we can do. The first step is

159

to become clear about why we have come to listen to the music. The second is to trust our ability to understand the music, to be caught up in it. The third is to give it our full awareness and attention, so that we allow the power of the music to trigger those deeper and subtler emotional responses which make music the almost magical force that it can be.

Step 1: Why do you listen to music?

Why do you listen to music? I am not talking about the music you hear in supermarkets or lifts, the background music that's designed to tranquillize us or sell us some new product: I am talking about the music you choose to listen to, the music that means something to you, that touches a special chord.

There are plenty of different reasons for going to a concert or putting a record on the stereo, and more than one of them may be motivating us on any particular occasion. Think about the different kinds of music you sometimes choose and notice your different reasons for choosing them:

- because you feel like dancing; to let your body move with the music;
- to accompany other activities: while you are working, perhaps, or driving in rush-hour traffic;
- to experience exaltation, to enrich your experience of life, to open yourself to the thoughts and feelings of Beethoven or Bessie Smith, Billy Joel or George Benson;
- to experience feelings such as anger, violence, jealousy, revenge or melancholy, which you normally find it difficult to feel, much less express, whether for social or personal reasons;
- to recall pleasant memories or call up a familiar feeling, or to experience a lift in mood when you're feeling lonely or depressed;
- to set a romantic atmosphere for the evening;
- to associate with those who share your interests, or

whose interests you would like to share – the opera buffs, the Punk kids, the ballet or jazz aficionados;

- to get out of the everyday routine;
- to learn more about kinds of music that you are unfamiliar with: bluegrass or madrigals, Balinese gamelan or the latest electronic wizardry from Philip Glass.

Our reasons for listening to music have a lot to do with how we feel when we finally get to the concert hall or plug in that new tape. If we go to a concert looking forward to being soothed and relaxed, only to discover that the music is dissonant and aggressive, we are likely to be disappointed.

Where is the meaning in music?

'This music is supposed to be great – so how come I'm not feeling inspired?' Many people who would like to listen to music ask themselves this question at one time or another. It means that one of two things is going wrong. Either they are listening in the wrong place or they are looking for a kind of meaning in music that just isn't there.

Does 'listening for the meaning in the music' seem to be difficult for you? Do you feel you don't know 'where to listen' or 'what to listen for'?

Throughout this book I have talked about listening to the meaning or feelings expressed in the music, but in a strictly philosophical sense that's inaccurate. The feeling and the meaning are certainly there in the composer while he's writing, and the music hopefully conveys them to the listener. But the listener feels or understands them in himself.

Some people find listening to music enormously frustrating, simply because they expect the feeling to be somehow outside them in the music itself. Just by switching their attention from the music to their own response to it, they will often find they are able to relax and enjoy music that was previously a frustration or a headache.

It sounds simple, and it is. It's one of those profoundly simple things that can make an enormous difference in the way you respond to music.

Another problem can arise if you've heard people talk about the 'meaning' in music and are listening for a kind of meaning that isn't there. Some music is called 'programme music' because it is intended to suggest a specific set of associations and responses in the listener. Beethoven's *Pastoral* Symphony, for instance, is intended to suggest the composer's own emotional response to an idyllic landscape, and includes musical mimicry of the sound of a cuckoo call and of the rippling waters of a small country stream.

Most music lacks this kind of specific detail and is written to communicate 'pure' emotions. The meaning of music is seldom something that could be expressed in words, and if you find you are 'listening for the meaning' without finding it, it may simply be that the word 'meaning' has misled you. Listen inside yourself for an emotional response in the way I described above – and you will be 'getting the meaning'.*

These two misunderstandings – that the feeling is somewhere outside you, or that the meaning ought to be something you could express in words – plague many listeners, who will find that music opens up new realms of meaning and feeling as soon as they let go of their worries and listen with an awareness of their own personal response to the music.

Choosing the music you know

When did you last attend a live concert? Did the music come up to your expectations? Go magnificently beyond them? Fall just that little bit short?

Remember the times you have felt disappointed or annoyed by a particular concert, record or tape. Sometimes, of course, the problem may have been that the record or tape was faulty, or that you didn't feel the conductor or soloist did a good job. But have there been times when your disappointment was due to the fact that what you wanted as a listener wasn't the same as what the composer and musicians intended to convey?

*Readers who would like to find more about the 'way in which music means' may wish to read J. W. N. Sullivan's short but wonderful book *Beethoven: His Spiritual Development*.

We are more likely to enjoy a concert if the music suits our moods and motivations, and this may mean we need to become familiar with the moods and feelings that different composers and pieces communicate so that we can select our listening the better to suit our tastes. We read movie reviews to find out which film we want to see; perhaps we'd do well to read up a little on the music we're going to hear.

Before you go to the concert, you may even want to get a copy of the programme and then buy a record of the music you'll be listening to (or borrow it from the library) so you can become familiar with it. Music you really 'know' can be much more vibrant for you in a live performance than music you are hearing for the first time.

Choosing new kinds of music

On the other hand, there's a tremendous excitement in finding out about music that we don't know about, that we 'wouldn't normally listen to'.

Flamenco guitar music at its best carries a haunting quality called 'duende', close cousin to the blues. A jazz musician may find the variations on a theme in Bach's C Minor Passacaglia and Fugue wonderful, and may recognize in Bach the kindred spirit and master of improvisation that he was. The Bach lover may find a friend in the twelve-string-guitar work of John Fahey. And the music lover whose tastes already range from Bartók to bebop may be astonished to discover Tibetan monastic music, the court music of Japan or the flute music of the native people of South America.

Many people tell me that they find the music of twentieth-century 'classical' composers hard to understand. Perhaps this is due in part to the tremendous variety of personal statements that composers as different as Benjamin Britten and Karlheinz Stockhausen wish to make, and partly to the new sounds and unfamiliar forms they use.

Most concertgoers prefer the 'old favourites' of the concert repertoire: Beethoven's *Eroica* and *Pastoral* symphonies, the Brahms Double Concerto, the *New World* Symphony of Dvořák, and Handel's *Messiah* at Christmas or Easter. These works remain popular partly because they are wonderful music, but also because people are familiar with them and can 'feel with them' more easily than with more recent works.

As a professional 'classical' musician, I know and love the works of Bach and Brahms, but I also know that Bach was better known as an organist than as a composer in his own lifetime, that Brahms sounded strange and new to his own contemporaries, and that Tchaikovsky's First Piano Concerto, now beloved of millions, was poorly received when it first appeared.

Obviously, not all the music composed today can be of this calibre. But it still makes sense to think that some of the works that tomorrow will be recognized as profound and beautiful masterpieces may be hard to appreciate at first hearing. Music that we find 'difficult' may be difficult simply because it's bad music, but it may also seem difficult because we need to learn to hear it if we are to discover the riches in it that later ages will recognize more easily.

There's much to be said for listening to the music you love the best, but there's also an incredible adventure in listening to new music and discovering areas of the musical spectrum from around the world that you never knew about.

Exercise: Listening goals

I have chosen to use Beethoven's Fifth Symphony for the exercises in this chapter, but if you would like to substitute a piece that is less familiar to you, maybe a 'difficult' modern piece, or a piece from a part of the musical repertoire that you are less familiar with, that's fine too.

1. Listen to the opening of Beethoven's Fifth. Imagine that Beethoven is making a personal statement with his music. Your only purpose in listening is to 'get' his message in sound. Did you feel you understood the meaning of the opening of this symphony?

2. Play the opening of the Fifth again, and this time pay attention not so much to the music as to the feelings it stirs up in you. Did the music come across more clearly this time? If it did, you may have just solved the problem of 'feeling' and 'meaning' in music and be well on your way to a more rewarding approach to listening.

3. Listen to the opening bars of the Fifth again, this time consciously deciding to do it for one of the reasons we listed under the heading 'Why do you listen to music?' Either

- allow your body to move with the music, or
- allow the music to release you from the humdrum routine of a day at the office, or
- use the music as a vehicle to deepen your emotions.

Did you find that clarifying your purpose in listening helped you to go more deeply into the music, or to get a better feel for what the composer wished to communicate?

4. Assess your mood and choose some music that fits your musical thirst at the moment. Play the piece that is somehow 'right' for the moment, whether it's an old favourite of yours or something new and challenging that will give you a sense of adventure and discovery.

Can you feel the difference between how you feel when you're 'not in the mood' for that kind of thing and the way you feel when this piece is 'right' for you?

Step 2: Trusting your ability to listen

Thousands of people who would never enter a concert hall flock to a classical concert in the park, where they can eat a picnic supper, lie on a blanket under the stars, and allow the music to work its magic on them. The relaxed atmosphere probably helps; it allows them to break through any doubts or fears they might have about their ability to listen and to open themselves to the music. Bringing that relaxed and open attitude into the concert hall can allow us to enjoy listening to music that we might not otherwise feel free to appreciate.

Trusting your experience of the music

We can only focus our conscious attention on a few things at a time, although Self 2 is capable of experiencing many different facets of music simultaneously.

If you have been technically trained in harmony, musical

form and orchestration, there are any number of technical aspects of the music that you can attend to while you are listening, but this can even be a distraction. Indeed, Professor Russell H. Miles, writing about the *St Matthew Passion* in his book *Johann Sebastian Bach: An Introduction to His Life and Works*, notes that a professional musician may 'hear more in this music, and therefore understand it better than a layman, but by the same token, he is more apt to become so engrossed in its technical wonders as to block off its access to his unconscious.' My own best listening experiences have always happened when I was directing my attention to only one or two elements in the music at a time.

On the other hand, even if you have no formal training in music, you have the ability to appreciate music and to become as absorbed in it as a formally educated musician. You have the advantage that technicalities cannot distract you from your feelings. You have the potential to see, hear, feel and understand.

In either case, trusting your experience while listening may mean paying attention to what you can see (or imagine), hear, feel and understand, or it may involve your appreciation of specific musical forms and techniques. The ability to step aside from doubt and confusion and entrust yourself to the music is something that each one of us is capable of.

Exercise: Entrusting yourself to the music

1. Think of the different environments in which you have listened to music. Have you listened to music in the park, at a school concert, on the stereo in your own room, in the car? Have you done some of these things with others or by yourself? Were you wearing formal 'concert' clothes or dressed more informally? Notice which of these settings had the biggest impact on your ability to listen freely and give yourself to the music. Which circumstances did you feel most comfortable in? Which ones do you associate with the occasions when you went the deepest into the music? Which environments do you prefer to listen in?

2. Play the first movement of Beethoven's Fifth again, in a private place where you won't be disturbed. Pretend you are

a great conductor standing on the podium. Notice how this affects your ability to hear and understand the music.

3. Now close your eyes, and while you listen to the second movement, pretend you are in your favourite listening environment. Does this allow you to let yourself go into the music more deeply?

4. This time listen to the third and fourth movements (the third runs directly into the fourth without a pause) and pretend you *are* the energy and emotions in the music. Let the power and emotion sweep through you as fully as possible. What do you feel? Are you experiencing aggression, power, strength, determination, anger, beauty?

5. Listen to the first movement again, noticing the opening theme and how it is introduced by various instruments in turn. Now imagine yourself talking to a six-year-old child about Beethoven's Fifth. Explain the way the various instruments introduce the theme. Notice how much you actually know about the piece as you are talking about it.

6. Close your eyes again and listen to the whole symphony as if you were living in Vienna in 1807. You have been a friend and companion of Beethoven's for years and know all his previous works for chamber groups, piano, orchestra and chorus. Listen with the pride that comes from knowing that this majestic music was written by your friend.

In the course of this exercise you may have found yourself hearing and feeling much more of the music than ever before. This ability to sense music deeply and to be caught up in it is present in you at all times, and it is only when external or internal distractions get in the way of it that listening becomes a frustration instead of the magical experience it can be.

Step 3: Using awareness to deepen your listening

The way to sidestep both external distractions (the kid chewing gum in the row in front) and internal ones (your doubt in your ability to concentrate, to follow the music or to understand a difficult piece) is to pay attention, using the awareness techniques of sight, sound, feeling and understanding.

If we allow Self 1 to analyse and criticize the music, or to doubt Self 2's ability to hear it, our awareness of the music will be interrupted, and we will miss the power of the composer's intention. Listening without judgement and with simple awareness puts us in the best position to take in the full impact of the music.

When we notice our attention has been distracted, we can choose to become aware of what we see, hear, feel, or know about the music. These techniques will heighten our awareness and increase our response to the music while also sidestepping interference and bringing us back to the present moment.

Our ultimate listening experiences happen when we are clear about our goals for listening, trust our ability to 'take in the music', and are completely present and aware of what we are hearing moment by moment.

Using visual awareness to enhance your listening

Paying attention to what you can see going on at a concert may not be essential if you are to enjoy the music, but it can be helpful. I have found I can sometimes see, hear and feel more of the music when I'm watching the conductor's gestures, or following the musicians' movements.

The conductor's right hand usually indicates the speed or tempo of a passage, but also sometimes emphasizes the character of 'feel' he is looking for. His left hand cues the musicians to their entrances, balances the level of sound and most importantly draws the feelings in the music out of the musicians. And his body language can also communicate a great deal about the music's energy and feeling. Watching a fine conductor at work can give you a sense of how the music is put together, carry you gently through lyric passages and sweep you up in the crescendos of the finale.

The principal players in the string sections of an orchestra use body signs to communicate with the other players in their section. Watching their head and shoulder movements can clue you in to the timing and character of an upcoming entrance.

String players' body movements give a phyical expression to the feeling of a phrase. If you watch how they prepare their arms and bodies to play, it can affect the way you listen to a melody. In the same way that I enjoy watching the linemen on a team carving a path for the fullback, I find it fascinating to watch musicians work as a team, communicating their music to the audience.

If you watch the string players' bows, you can pick up some other signals. The lower parts of the bow are used for a louder and more rhythmic effect, the middle of the bow is usually used for intricate passages, while the tip of the bow is used to express softer, more lyrical feelings.

Watch for the moments when players put mutes on their instruments – small extra pieces clipped on to the bridge of a violin, or conical devices placed in the business end of a trumphet or horn. Mutes change the colour and feeling of a piece.

Watching the percussion section can give you a warning of fireworks to come, particularly when a drummer stands up with the bass drum beater. You may recall the suspense in Hitchcock's film *The Man Who Knew Too Much*, when the entire plot hung on the moment when one man would stand up and clash the cymbals.

Noticing that extra musicians have joined the orchestra can help you to hear sounds that you might not have noticed otherwise. If eight horns, four bassoons, six trumpets and five trombones take the stage, it's likely that the wind and brass sections are going to play a crucial role in the performance.

Exercise: Watching the musicians

The next time you go to a concert, compare what you see with what you hear. Notice how the musicians reflect the character of the music in their gestures and expression. Allow your eyes to focus on different sections of the orchestra (strings, woodwind, brass, percussion, etc.), and particularly on the sounds created by the section you are watching.

Close your eyes and compare your experience with the experience you had while you were watching. Which taught you more? Which allowed you to go more deeply into the music?

Using visualization to create your own movie

Another way to use your visual sense to enhance your appreciation of music is to visualize, or make up imaginary movies in your head. You can do this by creating a story or simply by allowing yourself to 'see' images, colours or scenes that the music suggests to you. We saw in Chapter 5 how Charles increased the expressiveness of his performance of a Spanish guitar solo by narrating a story that dramatized the feelings within the music.

The connection between music and the visual arts has a long history. Specific paintings have often inspired composers. The composer Arnold Schoenberg was a close friend of the artist Kandinsky, and Schoenberg's music may become more accessible if you allow the brightly coloured, swirling forms of a Kandinsky abstract to float across the surface of your mind. Mussorgsky's piano suite *Pictures at an Exhibition* is another instance of paintings giving rise to music.

And the reverse is true, too: music has always evoked visual images. In his film *Fantasia* Walt Disney not only presented images evoked by music, but animated the patterns of music in several classical masterpieces. Music composed for the ballet and opera is often intended to evoke a visual response in the listener.

More recently, MTV has brought us visual images evoked by the lyrics of popular music. When the images effectively dramatize the story a song is telling and the feelings it expresses, they enrich our experience of the music as well.

Fantasia, the short clips on MTV, and 'programme pieces' like *Pictures at an Exhibition* can encourage us to 'direct' our own movies in the mind's eye and so deepen our experience of listening.

Exercise: Visualization

1. As you play the first movement of the Fifth on your stereo, picture Beethoven in your mind's eye, composing at his desk at home in Vienna in 1807. Imagine how he must have felt as he went to listen to the first rehearsal of his Fifth Symphony. He is almost totally deaf. Because he knocked over a choirboy holding some lighted candles at a previous rehearsal, he is not allowed to conduct, and he has to listen as best he can from the next room and report his comments and suggestions to the concertmaster at the end of each movement.

2. Now play the first movement again and imagine that the famous opening four-note theme represents groups of people arguing with one another. Imagine them sitting around a table, shouting the notes instead of words. As the music changes, imagine that different people are coming in and out and participating in the argument.

3. Play the same piece, but this time imagine that the different groups of notes are different swatches of colour. Substitute geometric shapes, or colours, or modern art forms for the different sounds. What do you see?

4. Imagine what the sounds of the orchestra would look like if they were portrayed on an oscilloscope, with a distinct shape for each note.

5. Create a story to accompany the Fifth, with actors, dancers and an appropriate background.

Which of these techniques did you learn most from? Which ones added most to your enjoyment of the music?

Using awareness of sound to enhance your listening

You may recall the exercise in Chapter 4 (p. 54) in which we focused on the sounds in the immediate environment. The purpose was to notice how other sounds tend to fade into the background when we focus on one sound at a time. This exercise shows you how you can avoid becoming irritated and distracted when you are listening to music and other sounds catch your attention: simply focus on the music and the distracting sounds will fade away. What follows is a variant on this exercise that can be very helpful for music listeners.

Exercise: Listening without judging

Take a moment to listen to the various sounds in the room. Isolate one sound, and just listen to it for a while . . .

What did you hear?

Did you identify the sound and name it? Did the thought 'That's the refrigerator [or the traffic, or whatever]' cross your mind? If you named it to yourself, did you hear the sound as clearly after you named it as before? Most people find that when they put a name to one of the sounds in their environment, they tend to pay less attention to it – and become more aware of the others.

Listen to the same sound again, but this time disregard what you think (or know) is causing it. Simply listen to the sound itself as pure sound.

Can you describe the texture of the sound (is it simple or complex?), its frequency (high or low), its beginning or ending? Does the sound change at all?

Do you notice any difference between the way you listened when you labelled the sound and the way you listened to it as pure sound without identifying and naming it?

I've found that when I listen to musical sounds without identifying them or putting them into categories ('Oh yes, the flute,' or 'There's the second theme'), I hear much more.

Non-judgemental awareness isn't just a matter of not having a negative response to the music you hear ('I don't like that flute tone.') It means pure awareness, free of any comment whatsoever. By simply listening to the sound of the music without even putting a name to what you're hearing, you may find yourself experiencing the music more deeply.

Listening to individual instruments

I had arranged to meet a jazz bass player friend in the club where he worked one day, and invited my friend Cindy Ellison to join me. The music made conversation a little difficult, and I discovered that Cindy didn't like jazz much anyway. 'It's too busy and too loud.' Cindy told me. 'I can't see any sense in it, and it makes me feel anxious and disorganized.'

I asked Cindy whether she would like to try some Inner Game listening techniques and suggested that she listen to the individual instruments in the band. The female vocalist was backed up by a piano, saxophone, bass and drums.

First we focused on the drummer, who was playing an entire battery of drums. I asked Cindy to isolate the lowest sound, the bass drum. She noticed the bass drum was complementing the string bass player and that they were both giving the music its basic energy, drive and rhythm. Then she picked out the sizzling sounds of two suspended cymbals and told me they were giving the group as a whole a distinct Latin sound. 'At first I thought the drummer was playing about ten instruments at once,' she told me, 'but I'm beginning to realize that he's giving each drum a different rhythm. I wonder how he keeps them all straight.'

We continued our experiment, listening only to the pianist's left hand, then to the bass playing the rhythm. We saw how the sax player used his shoulders for the higher notes. Cindy had become completely absorbed by now and she commented on the different styles the saxophonist used in different pieces. By the time I'd wrapped up my business with my bass friend and was ready to leave, Cindy was the one who wanted to stay for one more set.

The sound-awareness technique of listening selectively to specific voices can be applied to many kinds of music, from jazz to choral works and from string quartets to Mahler's *Symphony of a Thousand*.

Exercise: Focusing on the sound

1. Play the first movement of the Beethoven Fifth, focusing on one section of the orchestra at a time. Notice how the different instrumental groups alternate the four-note theme.

2. Notice the lengths and volumes of the notes played by the strings, the woodwinds, the brass instruments.

3. Pay attention to the unusual sound effects that are

created when Beethoven pairs particular instruments such as the violins and flutes or the bassoons and horns. Notice the way in which their sounds work together to create an entirely new texture.

4. Notice which instruments are playing the melody and which are supporting them with rhythmic chords. Notice the accents, the lengths of the notes, and the way that particular instrumental sounds change after they have been sounded (their resonance).

Did you find that by paying attention to individual sounds in this way, you understood more about Beethoven's orchestration? The complexity of his style?

Using feeling awareness to enhance your listening

Cindy had a fairly easy time isolating the various instruments in the jazz combo, but when it came to the singer, she felt confused and disoriented. The singer was vocalizing in 'scat' style – making vocal sounds without words that mimicked the style of a saxophone. 'It sounds like nonsense,' she told me.

I invited Cindy to relax, close her eyes, and imagine she was sitting in the front seat of a roller coaster. 'Notice how the singer raises and lowers her pitch by letting yourself ride the notes as if they were a roller coaster ride,' I suggested. 'Notice that some of the notes are fairly smoothly connected, and then there are the sudden dips and rises.' I was confident that when the notes went up, Cindy would imagine she was going uphill, and when they suddenly fell she would feel she was rushing down a slope. If the singer skipped around, the ride would become a little bumpy, and if she sang a smooth line, the ride would be flowing and smooth. 'Now hang on and go for a wonderful ride,' I said.

I could see Cindy's head bobbing and weaving. Her eyeballs were moving busily behind her lids. Her body began to sway with the music. Then the singing picked up speed and intensity. The scat began to skip, leap, twist, turn and fall. Cindy almost fell off her chair. 'What a ride,' she told me. 'That was wonderful. She's singing with fantastic skill and speed, and my body can barely keep up with her.'

Exercise: Riding the sound

1. Close your eyes and listen to the scherzo and trio of the Fifth Symphony. The melody is in the basses and cellos. Ride the music as if you were riding a roller coaster.

2. Allow your body to move with the direction and range of the melodic line. When the melody rises and falls, let your body move gently in sympathy.

3. Notice the stops in the trio and the changes in volume. Let the speed of your imaginary roller coaster be determined by the volume of the music.

How was the difference between the smooth ride in the scherzo, and the rougher ride in the trio?

Finding where the music resonates in your body

The pianist and composer Steven Halpern writes music that is designed to set a peaceful mood for relaxation, meditation and healing. He has researched the ways in which different musical vibrations affect different parts of the body, and reports that higher frequencies seem to register in the head, while lower sounds are 'felt' in the throat, chest or abdomen.

If you listen carefully, you can find where different notes register in your body. This technique allows your body as well as your mind to respond to the music and may increase your sense of involvement.

Exercise: Finding where the music resonates

1. Listen to the second (slow) movement of the Fifth and notice where you feel the music.

2. Do you feel the violins and flutes in your head? Your chest? Where do you feel them?

3. Where do you feel the violas and bassoons?

4. Where do you feel the basses and brass?

5. Does the music make you feel happy? Sad? Energetic? Angry? Romantic? Vibrant? Quiet?

6. Compare the way your body 'feels' the music with the emotional feeling it calls up in you. Are they the same or different? Do you sense that they work together to produce a total effect? What are you discovering about the ways in which you listen?

Playing along with the musicians

Another way to experience music in your body is to pretend you are one of the performers.

Tim Gallwey told me about a wonderful experience he had 'playing the music' along with the Apple Hill Chamber Players. They were performing a Brahms quartet for piano, violin, cello and clarinet. The music had plenty of energy and rhythm, and expressive melodic lines. Tim was not familiar with the form and structure of classical chamber music, but he could appreciate that he was witnessing a virtuoso performance.

He began to let his right hand move with the music, and found that his fingers were moving in sympathy with the bowing motions of the violinist. He couldn't anticipate every change of direction, but allowed the music to take muscular control of his hands. After a while, he switched his attention to the other instruments and his fingers responded to their different rhythms and melodies.

Soon the fingers of his left hand began to move in sympathy with the piano. He noticed the music was taking over his arms, shoulders, legs and body, and he had to restrain himself from standing up and conducting music he had never heard before. When he allowed his body to be open to the music in this way, he found that not only his fingers but his emotions, too, were powerfully engaged.

Exercise: Playing along with the musicians

1. Listen to the last movement of the Fifth Symphony. Allow the fingers of your left or right hand to move with the melody in the brass and strings.
2. Allow your other hand to move with the voices of the rhythmic instruments.
3. Let your head move with the faster notes.
4. When you feel ready, let your arms move with the energy of the piece.
5. If you feel like it, stand up and allow your whole body (shoulders, back, hips, legs, feet) to move in any direction that expresses the music. Let yourself conduct like a maestro – or dance.

Using understanding to enhance your listening

A work of art is only interesting and absorbing for us when we become involved in what the artist is communicating – when it begins to touch us personally. This involvement occurs primarily through the senses and the emotions. But an intellectual grasp of what led up to the writing of a particular piece, or the composer's intentions for it, can also enrich our listening. It can give us clues about what to listen for and allow us to catch subtleties and nuances that we would otherwise miss.

You may feel that your listening to the Fifth gains in depth when you know a little more of the story of the work. Ludwig van Beethoven was born in 1770. By the time he composed his Fifth Symphony in 1807, he was already struggling with the loss of his hearing. Five years before, in 1802, he had written, 'I must live like an exile . . . What a humiliation when one stood beside me and heard a flute in the distance, and I heard nothing. Such incidents brought me to the verge of despair.'

Deafness was a terrible fate for him, and Beethoven said of the Fifth, 'I will grapple with Fate; it shall not overcome me.'

Beethoven is supposed to have said of the first four notes, 'Thus Fate knocks at the door.' This four-note theme of impending doom is finally overcome in the opening of the final movement, when the C minor chord turns to C major.

Beethoven was a short, stout man with a very red face, small, piercing eyes, bushy eyebrows and a mane of white hair flowing over his broad shoulders. He was often criticized for his sudden shifts of emotion – and the unpredictability of his music. He was also an innovative composer and introduced the trombone into symphonic music for the first time in the finale of the Fifth, a work in which he also used the piccolo and contrabassoon.

His music expresses his innermost struggles, and if you listen to the Fifth with an appreciation for the way he must have felt about his approaching deafness, the volcanic, exuberant, impulsive and unrelenting power of the music may reach you even more deeply.

You may also find it helpful to know that Beethoven was a great admirer of Napoleon. Something of the grandeur of this symphony may derive from Beethoven's wish to express his admiration for this victorious general who had crowned himself Emperor in 1804.

Exercise: Using understanding to enhance your listening

1. See how much struggle and conflict you can sense in the first movement of the Fifth. Can you feel Beethoven struggling with his deafness? Do you hear him reaching out? Can you feel the tension?

2. As you listen to the second movement, notice the contrast with the mood of the first. Feel how the movement builds to a forceful climax. Beethoven was breaking with symphonic tradition when he ended this movement in tension and anxiety. Can you sense this anxiety, and the drive Beethoven must have felt in him to dispense with tradition in this way?

3. Notice how the energy builds in the scherzo and trio. Can you hear how the drumbeats interrupt the momentum?

Does this music prepare you for the transition to the finale?

4. As you listen to the last movement, can you hear the trombones? Notice the power and finality of the last chords. Is anything left undone, unsaid?

12 Parent and coach

There are few things as wonderful as watching the growth of one's child or pupil and being able to play a role in his or her development. Sometimes a brief comment from a parent or teacher can encourage a pupil to new heights. New musical visits may also open when a child discovers a new composer, attends a special concert, obtains a new instrument, wins an audition or receives an award.

The reverse is, unhappily, all too often the case. When a parent or coach withholds trust from a pupil, or when the pupils are themselves discouraged by a poor showing in an exam or recital, the result can be devastating. A musical child who is taunted by classmates for spending time practising or for listening to kinds of music that their peers perceive as unfashionable or snobbish may decide it is easier to 'close down' than to continue under pressure, thereby losing access to a vital source of delight and self-expression.

Here are three ways in which a supportive relationship can be developed beteen a parent or coach and a child or pupil:

1. Acknowledge growth and encourage the pupil's trust in his or her musicianship.

2. Help the pupil to establish clear and appropriate goals in the areas of performance, experience and learning.

3. Expand the pupil's musical awareness in the areas of sight, sound, feeling and understanding.

Acknowledgement and trust

Some years ago Harvard psychologist Robert Rosenthal ran an experiment that explored the impact teachers can have on their students' subsequent performance. In Dr Rosenthal's study a group of teachers were informed that the 'less gifted' students entering their classes were 'more gifted', and vice versa. After a while the teachers' encouragement of the students they imagined were more intelligent began to have an effect: the students who had been labelled 'more gifted' began to outscore their 'less gifted' peers.

Dr Rosenthal coined the term 'the Pygmalion Effect' to describe this sudden flowering of pupils, previously considered low achievers, when they received encouragement and support from their teachers. As a result of Dr Rosenthal's studies it is now widely recognized in education that our expectations about how others will perform may have at least as much of an impact on their subsequent achievement as any other single factor.

Acknowledgement rather than judgement

In almost every phase of our lives – at home, in school or at work – we find ourselves alternately encouraged and discouraged by an almost continuous stream of opinions, words of praise and criticism, rewards and punishments. Phrases such as 'You've blown it again', 'That was very good', 'This is really difficult', 'You have to remember', and 'Will you never learn' still echo in my mind from my own childhood, and every one of us has heard them more times than we care to remember.

It's evident from the results of the Rosenthal study quoted above that a teacher or parent who has little faith in a child's ability to learn can transmit doubts to the child. Critical comments and judgements such as 'That sounded terrible' reinforce the pupil's tendency to insecurity and self-doubt. But it isn't enough simply to 'find something positive to say'. Even seemingly positive comments like 'That sounded terrific' can contribute to a child's anxiety when used manipulatively.

Your enthusiasm and encouragement are of tremendous value to the young musicians, and even evaluations can be helpful – as long as they strengthen the individual's own sense of purpose and growth. The following examples may give you an idea of how to avoid making value judgements and authoritative pronouncements, while acknowledging your child or pupil's growth and expressing your enthusiasm and concern.

Judgement Version:	Non-judgemental Phrasing:
The piece is too difficult for you.	How difficult do you feel this piece would be for you on a 1-to-10 scale? Is it a little beyond your reach at the moment, or do you think you can handle it?
It sounded terrible.	Keep it up and listen carefully to the pitch in bars 2 and 5.
That was great!	I could really feel your expression. I loved it!

Becoming aware of the way you phrase your comments is a big part of the battle, and I still catch myself from time to time using phrases that make my students feel self-conscious rather than encouraged. But your attitude can express itself in other ways besides words, and simply 'adapting' your verbal comments from a 'judgemental' to a 'non-judgemental' format may not be enough.

Children are peculiarly sensitive to the attitudes of those around them, and your quite natural keenness to see your child or student succeed may pose a problem if the child begins to feel the purpose of playing is to please others. When parents or coaches emphasize the importance of practice, study or musical performance to children, they risk having the children feel they are playing or practising solely to win approval. Even a parent's or coach's concern for the child's own experience can have this effect. It is wonderful for students to enjoy their practice, but less wonderful if they feel obliged to do so.

Letting your students or children know you accept them the way they are will allow them to explore without feeling constantly under pressure to measure up to some standard. You can help your children and students to develop and retain their own understanding of their progress by

1. remaining calm and confident before and during performance;

2. asking your student or child after the performance about their own experience: 'How did you feel about the music?'

3. avoiding judgement;

4. expressing your own experience and feelings: 'I really noticed and enjoyed the subtle ending you gave the piece.'

5. acknowledging the growth that you see from performance to performance.

The best way to acknowledge what a child or student has learned in practice and performance is by asking them what they felt they accomplished. Students who verbalize what they have learned reaffirm and strengthen their new knowledge in the process, and become more confident and trusting as a result.

Adult beginners

As we have seen, many adults who take up an instrument set extraordinary (and unfairly) high standards for themselves and can be quite unaware of the very real progress they are making as a result. I quite often come across flautists who are already comparing their playing unfavourably with Jean-Pierre Rampal or James Galway. These comparisons inevitably block the beginners' awareness of their own sound.

When the coaches can lead adult beginners away from this kind of comparison and back to an experience of their week-by-week progress, the players will often be surprised and delighted to recognize the real advances that they are making.

Co-operation rather than competition

The Suzuki method for teaching young children to play violin, piano and other instruments develops trust and confidence in these young musicians through group lessons and recitals. Parents and classmates become a support system, and the group lessons and recitals are showcases in which the pupils can share what they have learned and show others where they are going. More advanced pupils become role models for their younger colleagues, and the selections they play help the younger players to form their musical tastes and goals.

I was recently privileged to watch a violin workshop led by Suzuki instructor Craig Timmerman. I found that he was able to instill trust and confidence in his four- to six-year-old students by acknowledging what they had just learned and then spurring them on to even greater accomplishments.

The piece was 'Twinkle, Twinkle, Little Star'. Craig played the beginning of the melody, then changed the starting pitch so the kids were forced to transpose the line to another string or position. He didn't tell them what fingers to use or which notes had changed, but the kids just followed along, playing by ear. Somehow they managed to make the necessary adjustments.

Craig told the children he'd noticed they 'played that in a different key', and asked them how they'd managed to do it. One child enthusiastically explained the process by which he'd made the jump from one key to another.

Then another remarkable thing happened. Craig played the entire piece with the kids, including the middle section, which he had never demonstrated or played for them: the kids simply figured it out for themselves. 'Wait a minute,' Craig told them, 'you can't do that – I didn't teach you the middle section yet.' The children had a 'we don't know how we did it' look on their faces. Craig asked them, 'Who told you how that middle section goes?' and no one could answer him. 'That's amazing, what you just did,' Craig continued. 'I can't believe my ears. You played that without my help. Wasn't that fun? You really have a special gift inside you that tells you things you don't even know!'

Craig Timmerman makes sure he acknowledges what the children have learned. They respond with an added trust in themselves and leave the class inspired to continue their practice and enjqyment of music.

The need for clear goals

Parents and coaches can help their children and students a great deal by helping them form clear musical goals.

1. Performance goals

It is helpful for a child or pupil to have a feel for how the music should sound before he or she attempts to play it. This doesn't, of course, mean that children are 'supposed' to play the music exactly the way it's performed on a particular record or tape, but it does mean that an aquaintance with the music will help them to understand what they are hoping to achieve. Making records and tapes of solos and études available to students (whether by purchasing them or by obtaining them from your local library) can be a real help.

A portable cassette player can be an invaluable gift to young students. It allows them to listen to the music they are going to play and can also be used to record lessons, thus serving as a reminder of their learning and performance goals for the week.

Taking students or children to professional and student recitals is another way to encourage them in their musical goals. If families watch and listen to TV-FM simultaneous broadcasts of concerts, this can provide children with much-needed musical experience in the context of warm family support. Listening to both live and recorded music will enlarge the pupils' taste, style and repertoire and elevate their standards of learning and performance.

Encouraging your child or pupil to keep a musical journal will help them to keep track of what they learned in one lesson and what they will be playing in the next.

It may seem obvious, but parents can encourage and inspire a child to practise by providing good instruments and an attractive space and atmosphere in which to practise. In physical terms this is likely to mean providing appropriate chairs, stands, a metronome and good lighting. Even more important, perhaps, it means respecting your child's practice time.

2. *Experience goals*

Some children love to practise; others don't. The key here is to ensure that your child enjoys the actual experience of music making as much as possible. When students have a good time while they are learning, they not only learn more – they perform better, too. Structuring a time during each practice session that is devoted to the student's delight in learning and playing (described in Chap. 9, p. 141) will strengthen his or her goals in the area of enjoying and feeling the music he or she plays.

I have already talked a little about Craig Timmerman's violin lesson. The lesson I described was part of a Suzuki method workshop at which eight excellent cello and violin teachers from regional states demonstrated the Suzuki approach.

These eight teachers each had a different personal style of teaching, and I noticed that the more humour there was in a class, the better the results, and that the teachers who 'taught' and lectured least had the most success with their students. The younger players were less enthusiastic about learning the 'whys, dos, and don'ts' than they were about playing and enjoying their music – and in my experience most adults feel the same way.

Craig Timmerman's class seemed more like a 'play session' than a group lesson. Craig would play a tune on his violin, and a child would then play a variation of his own. Then the children would play a tune, and Craig would play it back to them, making fun of it by slurring some of the notes, playing some of the others pizzicato, and so on. He would encourage them to play the melody in a variety of different styles – slower, faster, happily, sadly, gracefully and then clumsily, lazily and with dynamic energy. Sometimes he would deliberately play wrong notes, and the children would take a gleeful delight in correcting him. There was a minimum of thinking and talking, and a maximum of music making.

The kids enjoyed laughing at themselves instead of being judged for their mistakes. They learned quickly and seemingly effortlessly, while playing musical games, and Craig acknowledged even the smallest improvement in each child's playing.

Making practice more fun

We have already described some of the ways in which you can make a practice session more enjoyable by setting aside a time in each session (or even a whole session) for experimentation, creativity and play. If your child is playing a classical piece, setting aside some time to improvize in a jazz style may give him or her real freedom of expression and technique, flexibility and added confidence. Inevitably, practice involves discipline and repetition, but there's no reason why it shouldn't also include exploration and delight.

You can encourage your child to enjoy practice time by making a small investment in equipment. Both Casio and Yamaha now manufacture electronic keyboards and small synthesizers that are available for prices in the one-hundred-dollar range. These instruments allow your child or pupil to switch the rhythm control (a percussion synthesizer) to a variety of settings such as rock, waltz, samba, swing, pop or disco. This can make the playing of scales, arpeggios, études and some sonatas 'swing'. Some of the instruments also include variable pitch control, which allows the student to 'tune' the keyboard to your home stereo system.

You can also buy records and cassette tapes of popular string orchestra accompaniments to your pupil's études, sonatas, symphonies and even concertos. Some of these recordings are sold under the title 'Music Minus One'; they allow the student to practise a solo part while accompanied by an entire ensemble.

A variable pitch cassette recorder is another investment

that's worth considering. It allows students to tune a tape to their own instruments instead of the reverse, and also means that they can practice music transposed to other keys. There are also many jazz and popuar music 'methods' which include LP or taped accompaniments for the young learner.

The computer is also rapidly becoming a valuable aid to musicians. New software is now appearing on the market that helps teach the student music fundamentals, orchestration, sight-reading, ear training, harmony, improvisation and composition.

Suzuki World's *Ability Development Catalogue* lists a wide variety of books, cassettes, music, accessories and electronic aids for parents and musicians. You can obtain it by writing to Ability Development, Box 4260, Athens, OH 45701.

Exercise: Discovering characters and stories in music

My friend and Suzuki piano colleague Peggie Luey has found that encouraging her pupils to discover the 'personalities' of the different themes in a piece and to create a drama or story about the music that are playing adds life and enjoyment to the music.

1. Play this piece without any emphasis on the feelings that the written score implies.

2. Link the words of the text with the musical phrases and allow your feeling for the text to change your dynamics, rhythm, tone and energy.

3. Now imagine the different phrases as different people. You might like to talk about them with your parent or teacher until you feel you 'know' them. Now play the piece again, this time allowing these characters to 'speak' through you, perhaps even building a story that involves your characters.

4. Pick another piece of your own choosing and repeat this exercise.

SICILIANO

R. Schumann

Practice and motivation

Many children, happily, don't need any encouragement to practise: their own excitement at learning music, together with the positive support they receive from teachers and family, is enough. But as children grow and change, there may be times when further motivation is necessary. Learning music involves commitment and discipline; patience and practice are indispensable.

When younger children lose touch with their enjoyment of practice, offering them a reward for regular and consistent work may help. But these rewards need to be of a kind that the child genuinely enjoys. Peggie Luey found that allowing her very active and fidgety five-year-old student a run around the studio was an appropriate reward for a piece well learned. She also told me that parties after recitals and "I Played It 100 Times" buttons provided her six- and seven-year-old students with the motivation to keep on practising. Incentives such as workshops, music camps and tickets to concerts can help to motivate older children and young adults to accept the responsibility for disciplined practice.

I must admit that I feel a little hesitant about offering rewards for regular practice, however. I can certainly suggest it as a method of dealing with those times when a child feels temporarily reluctant to practise, perhaps because their lives are filled with so many other interests and occupations. But rewards of this sort are temporary at best. The best motivation for practising music is enjoying the process of learning and making music.

Playing with others

Playing with others in small groups, chamber orchestras, jazz combos, and school, county or regional bands is a way to experience many of the delights of music in a supportive atmosphere. It encourages students to learn more about music and to attain higher levels of technical and musical proficiency. Parents and coaches may well find that taking the time and effort to provide their children or students with this kind of social and musical interaction pays off in terms of increased enthusiasm and learning.

Playing for others

Young players can often benefit from opportunities to share their musical experiences. The parent or coach who would like to structure this kind of opportunity needs to be creative about it. The possibilities include arranging a weekly family concert, playing at church or in the class recital, or performances at a local nursing or retirement home.

I remember as a child fetching my accordion every time I heard the front doorbell ring, in the hopes that I would get a chance to share what I'd learned in my latest practice. When children get the opportunity to share what they have learned with others, it allows them to demonstrate the completion of even a seemingly small task – and we should remember that what seems small to us may be a terrific achievement to the children. When we can acknowledge these achievements with opportunities for children to perform, we are not only encouraging new growth, but also building confidence and trust.

3. Learning goals

As we saw in Chapter 10, the best way to learn is by means of your own awareness and experience. We shall therefore discuss the enhancement of learning goals under our third major heading:

Awareness

A parent or coach can structure lessons or practice sessions so that the pupil's awareness is engaged in the areas of sight, sound, feeling and understanding.

One way to increase children's visual awareness is to ask them to describe what they are looking at while they are playing. Here are some examples that may lead to further visual awareness:

'Can you see the position your bow is in?'
'Where are your fingers when you hear that funny sound?'
'Can you point to the dynamic markings in the music?'
'Can you see the circle your bow makes as you play?'
'Check your position.'
'Point to the place where my position is awkward.'
'Does it look right?'
'Where is your elbow now?'
'Are you watching your fingers?'
'Did you notice all the rests in the music?'

Sound awareness is also important. It can give children the feedback they need to be able to adjust their playing when dealing with a difficult technical problem. Here are some questions that encourage sound awareness:

'Are you ahead of the piano or behind it when you play those semi-quavers?'

'Can you still hear all the little notes when you play faster?'

'Can you sing the music you are playing?'

'Can you hear both voices clearly?'

'Is this your softest sound?'

'Were you listening to the pitch during the change of register?'

'Can you hear "air in the sound"?'

'Does it sound like the bow is stuck to the string?'

Feeling awareness can be encouraged by drawing the pupil's attention to the way their bodies feel while they are playing. Helpful questions might include:

'How is the posture of your back?'

'How does your arm feel when you're playing those rapid passages?'

We discussed another way to increase feeling awareness in Chapter 7 (p. 111) under the heading 'Doing Something Familiar'. The idea is to suggest images of movements from other areas of activitiy that resemble the movements involved in playing music. Percussionists can sometimes understand a wrist motion if I compare it to the motion of screwing in a light bulb, or to a cobra striking.

Motions of the bow can be compared to bouncing a basketball, or pretending the bow is stuck to the string by a magnet.

A sliding motion on the keyboards can be compared to roller-skating.

The pulse of the music can be compared to the rhythm of riding a horse, and you can invite your child's whole body to move with it.

Imagining that there's a heavy towel on your wrist can heighten sensitivity to weight in the fingertips and wrists.

Keyboard players can be enouraged to heighten their sensitivity by pretending their fingers are the legs of a caterpillar.

Asking students to pretend there are springs in their fingers can help promote flexibility.

Feeling imaginary 'hinges' in their arms can help them to locate the parts that need to be flexible, and pretending there is oil in their joints can help keep them limber.

The air flowing through a singer's throat can be compared to a breeze in a canyon.

Children can overcome wind resistance by imagining they are blowing out the candles on a cake.

Lastly, awareness with understanding can enhance a pupil's interest in and feeling for the music they are playing. Knowing roughly what the music should sound like is essential, if children are to be able to give shape, structure and meaning to the music they play. Parents can facilitate this kind of awareness by providing records and tapes and by taking their child to concerts. Musical encyclopedias and books about composers can open up new vistas for younger performers. Sometimes an English, social studies or history project can give students a chance to increase their musical knowledge while bringing their enthusiasm to bear on a different aspect of their studies.

Maximal awareness comes about when the pupil is able to draw on all these avenues of experience. Parents and coaches are most helpful when they create an environment where students can learn by means of what they see, hear, feel and know – and be supported and acknowledged for it.

13 Integration and balance

The conductor George Szell remarked, 'In music one must think with the heart and feel with the brain.' Musicians are divided in their opinion on many subjects, and some musicians seem temperamentally inclined to emphasize thought over feeling or heart over brain.

Some of us prefer passion, and some prefer restraint. Some prefer our music disciplined, while for others a sense of freedom is more important. Some of us value authenticity and order, and some prefer deeply felt expression. There are those who value their emotional experience most, and those who value a strong critical and analytical approach. There are intuitive musicians, and there are those whose playing is grounded in music history and the theory of composition.

Both approaches certainly have much to offer, but in the final analysis, some balance between them is needed. Someone who hammers away enthusiastically at the piano keys without any discipline or sense of order is unlikely to produce music; the player whose fingering and technique are perfect but who lacks all feeling sounds dry and academic. To some extent, at least, we must learn to integrate our feelings and our technique, our discipline and our sense of musical freedom. George Szell has said: 'think with the heart and feel with the brain.'

The two hemispheres of the brain

During the past twenty years, great advances have been made in brain research, and one of the most fascinating findings has been the discovery that the two hemispheres of the neo-cortex, the distinctively human part of the brain, can function independently.

For a while it looked as though the two hemispheres worked according to two very different principles – the left hemisphere functioning logically and rationally, and mainly dealing with thought in terms of words and numbers, the right hemisphere working intuitively and metaphorically, mainly dealing with images and relationships. If you like, the 'left brain' was thought to be 'disciplined' and 'rigorous', while the 'right brain' was seen as more 'intuitive' and 'emotional'.

Howard Gardner of Harvard's Project Zero deals with the question of the 'two brains' and our current understanding of their relationship to music in his excellent look *Art, Mind and Brain*. He discusses a number of recent experiments and concludes that 'it is far too simple to conclude that music is principally a right-brain function.'

Whatever our final understanding of the way the brain works turns out to be, the early experiments in split-brain research certainly led to a useful distinction between two ways in which humans go about the business of putting information together, which we can usefully term the 'analytical' and 'global' styles. The analytic style characteristically deals with information by sorting out the individual components and putting them in order, while the global style prefers to see things in context and to understand the ways in which the whole is greater than the sum of its parts.

As you would have undoubtedly noticed, these two approaches correspond pretty closely to the two kinds of musicians we discussed above – those who emphasize accuracy and displine, and those who find emotion and intuition more important than accuracy.

Most people have a natural inclination towards one of these two styles, and both our musical preferences and our styles of learning and performing music are likely to reflect that inclination. Our taste, preferences and choices are often influenced by such things as the social, political or spiritual values we hold, by our past training and family background. In order for us to balance the two approaches, we need to find out which approach we tend to favour.

To help you get a sense of which style you feel most comfortable with, I have made a loose adaptation of three or four tests that were devised at a time when it was thought that these two styles or approaches, the global and the analytical, were characteristic of the two hemispheres of the brain. The original tests were designed to identify 'left- or right-brain dominance'. With some modifications to bring them to bear on the subject of music, they work equally well as a test of which of the two styles you tend toward.

Before you start the test, though, I'd like to make it clear that there are no 'right' answers. Both strongly 'analytical' and strongly 'global' personalities have their strengths and weaknesses, which will show up in music. The questions that follow are simply meant to offer you an insight into your way of dealing with situations, not to suggest that one method is better or worse than another.

Test for analytical or global preference

Read through the statements that follow, and in each case make a check mark against the answer which you prefer. Give only one answer to each question, and take your time.

1. I respond better when people appeal
   (a) to my logical side and my intellect ( )
   (b) to my emotional side and my feelings ( )
   (c) no preference ( )
2. When I listen to music, I like to
   (a) analyse its structure, and take pleasure in accuracy and detail ( )
   (b) receive its emotional impact, and take pleasure in my overall response ( )
   (c) no preference ( )
3. I consider myself
   (a) primarily intellectual ( )
   (b) primarily intuitive or emotional ( )
   (c) no preference ( )
4. I prefer to learn
   (a) facts and details, piece by piece and measure by measure ( )

197

(b) from a general overview, by seeing the piece as a whole ( )

(c) no preference ( )

5. I prefer to be taught
    (a) verbally, by means of explanation ( )
    (b) non-verbally, by being shown what to do ( )
    (c) no preference ( )

6. I like to
    (a) solve one problem at a time ( )
    (b) work on several things at once ( )
    (c) no preference ( )

7. I like
    (a) master classes where I can listen and take notes ( )
    (b) informal classes where I can try things out ( )
    (c) no preference ( )

8. I make my decisions
    (a) by taking an objective look at the facts ( )
    (b) by subjectively evaluating my feelings ( )
    (c) no preference

9. I prefer my lessons and practice to be
    (a) structured, so I know exactly what my goals are, and what to do ( )
    (b) spontaneous, so that I have a chance to change things as I go along ( )
    (c) no preference ( )

10. When there's a technical problem, I
    (a) like to know the recommended solution ( )
    (b) like to be inventive and play my hunches ( )
    (c) no preference ( )

11. I work with a
    (a) disciplined, linear, businesslike approach ( )
    (b) playful, non-linear, free-form approach ( )
    (c) no preference ( )

12. I learn best with teachers who
    (a) explain how things work directly ( )
    (b) play and demonstrate things for me ( )
    (c) no preference ( )

13. I prefer
    (a) to make something better ( )
    (b) to create or invent something ( )

(c) no preference   ( )

14. I usually
    (a) organize my time carefully   ( )
    (b) have difficulty setting time limits ( )
    (c) no preference   ( )
15. I have
    (a) very few mood changes   ( )
    (b) many mood periods   ( )
    (c) no preference   ( )
16. I prefer the music of
    (a) Bach   ( )
    (b) Brahms   ( )
    (c) no preference   ( )
17. I prefer to discover the style of a piece by
    (a) doing research, listening to recordings ( )
    (b) trusting my instincts   ( )
    (c) no preference   ( )
18. I am
    (a) usually punctional   ( )
    (b) sometimes absentminded   ( )
    (c) no preference   ( )
19. I like to solve problems by
    (a) taking them apart and systematically
    restructuring them   ( )
    (b) seeing the problem as a whole and using
    experimentation based on my hunches ( )
    (c) no preference   ( )
20. I prefer
    (a) scholarly interpretations of music ( )
    (b) emotional interpretations of music ( )
    (c) no preference   ( )
21. I'd rather study theory, harmony and analysis
    (a) before learning a piece   ( )
    (b) after learning the piece   ( )
    (c) no preference   ( )
22. I prefer
    (a) multiple choice tests   ( )
    (b) essay examinations   ( )
    (c) no preference   ( )

Now add up the total number of times you checked an (a) answer, and the total number of times you checked a (b). If you tended to answer most questions with an (a), you have a tendency to prefer the 'analytical' approach, while if you mostly answered (b), you favour the 'global' approach. If you chose the (c) response much of the time, or if your answers favoured (a) and (b) about equally, you tend to use a balance of the two approaches.

As I suggested above, there are no right or wrong answers in these matters. We all use both approaches all the time and could hardly play music at all if we didn't. The point is that those who favour one mode over the other will tend to rely more heavily on it when problems arise, and it can be useful to know this and to exercise the weaker of the two styles of approach.

Let's take a look at the characteristics of these two modes of functioning and see how they operate in terms of playing music.

The analytical mode

Sequential order and physical movement are regulated by those parts of the brain that govern analytical function. It is our 'analytical' mode of functioning which produces and controls our articulations and bowing attacks – the beginnings and endings of notes. The analytical mode ensures that we play the correct notes in the correct order and with proper rhythm, telling the body exactly what to do and when to do it. It only processes one item at a time and doesn't see the parts of the piece in relation to the whole.

Analytical functioning is also responsible for the memorization of muscle movements. We don't have to think about it when we retrieve the car key from our trousers pocket, insert it into the ignition and release the brake; the same kind of memory of sequential patterns and physical movements allows us to repeat scales, recognize rhythms and play with correct pitch without having to relearn a piece every time we play it.

The global mode

By contrast, we use those parts of the brain that govern global function to obtain intuitive insights into the style, emotions and meaning of the music we play. It is our 'global' mode of functioning which provides the creative, dramatic and interpretive qualities of our performance, and these in turn bring spontaneity and flexibility to our playing. Global functioning is aware of the sense of the whole piece, while dealing with individual notes and phrasings. More specifically, global functioning controls the delicate adjustments of fingering that make accurate pitch possible on string instruments.

Self 1 and Self 2

When I describe the qualities of Self 1 and Self 2 to my friends and colleagues, their response is often to compare them with right- and left-brain functioning, or to the analytical and global approaches. As we have seen, the early picture of right- and left-brain functioning as virtually synonymous with the global and analytical styles has been modified by recent research.

Self 1 is not a new name for the left brain, nor for the analytical function; neither is Self 2 just another way of describing the right brain, or the global approach. Let's go back to the definitions of Self 1 and Self 2 which we adopted in Chapter 2 (p. 29). We said there that:

●   if it interferes with your potential, it's Self 1, and
●   if it's your potential expressing itself, it's Self 2.

Self 1 interference can interfere with left and right brains, with analytical and global functioning, and your Self 2 potential includes both sides of the brain and both your global and analytical modes of functioning.

Revaluing the two approaches

The tradition of music education as it has developed over the last hundred years or so has tended to emphasize the logical and analytical functions over those that are global and emotional. The violin methods of Ivan Galamian and Carl Flesch, for instance, are based on systematic principles of muscular movement and training, and emphasize discipline and accuracy in learning and playing music.

Emphasis on analytical skills has been so widespread in general during this period that many of us feel inhibited about developing and utilizing our 'global' and creative side. Perhaps this is why so many children begin to lose their spontaneity and creativity at about the same time that they are acquiring the sequential and logical skills associated with the analytical approach. Many of us wind up feeling that we are unable to be expressive and creative, and that we lack intuition, imagination and playfulness.

Many young musicians lose their enthusiasm for music as their education places more and more emphasis on analytical functioning and less and less on the global approach. This loss of enthusiasm can be made worse by strong pressure from the young person's peers: teenage boys are often made to feel that it's 'unmasculine' to want to play the violin or flute, and teenage girls that it is correspondingly 'unfeminine' to want to play the trumpet, trombone, bass, percussion or low woodwinds.

By emphasizing the importance of such 'global' functions as spontaneity, creativity, intuition and feeling, and balancing these functions with their analytical equivalents – discipline, logic and accuracy – we can enlarge our approach to the teaching and learning of music. The more we come to understand about these two approaches, the easier it will be for us to recognize where our music is out of balance and to draw on the appropriate mode, whether analytical or global, to handle the situation and arrive at a successful integration of both.

I recently conducted a small experiment to discover what musicians could gain from emphasizing the analytical and global approaches separately and then together, and discovered that learning to recognize and develop the two approaches separately made it much easier for players than adopting an integrated balance of the two.

Dan, a viola player, played for me a Baroque sonata by Telemann. I asked him to play his solo a second time with precise rhythm and accurate dynamics – as if he were a robot or computer. If the score indicated piano (*p*), he was to play at that level until the next dynamic (*f*), and shift immediately to forte at that point. If a crescendo was marked, he should begin the crescendo precisely on the first note and increase his volume steadily until the last. I told him to concentrate on mechanical precision and suggested there was no need for him to add any warmth or expression to the sound (for instance, through the use of vibrato).

The result was both interesting and surprising. Dan managed to make the music sound inhuman and mechanical to the point of complete blandness – but his playing contained many positive qualities that his original performance had lacked. His rhythm was accurate and clear; his pitch improved remarkably. His hand positions were more accurate, thus allowing him to manage a purer tone. His physical handling of his viola was more formal and controlled than usual.

Dan recognized these improvements and realized that, by emphasizing the analytical side and putting his attention on performing with accuracy and discipline, he had strengthened these areas.

We then explored the global approach together. I told Dan to ignore technique and accuracy and to play only from his heart, his feelings and his understanding of the music. I suggested that Dan regard the dynamic markings simply as suggestions. I asked him to produce a tone like that of the human voice and to let each phrase express emotion; I suggested that he play spontaneously and playfully, and feel free to be experimental in his interpretation. He could ignore the printed articulations, slurs and bowings, stretch the dynamics and allow his rhythm to be less precise.

This produced another interesting performance. This time Dan's playing was exaggerated, gushy, and lacked pitch, rhythm and accuracy; he sounded as if he were a little drunk. At the same time, Dan was playing with a new sense of freedom and was 'giving himself to the music' to a greater extent than before.

Then I asked Dan to combine the appropriate qualities of the two approaches. After the first few bars his music began to take a new shape. His rhythm and pitch were accurate, while he was still able to play expressively and with feeling. He blended the dynamics from one phrase to the next. His attacks (bow changes) were well placed, while his tone and vibrato gave meaning to the phrases.

As the piece developed, Dan's playing picked up new energy. He played the faster passages in character, yet accurately. The notes, rhythms, pitches and delightful phrasings succeeded one another, developing and deepening to a satisfying conclusion. Dan's performance was stunning in its accuracy and its feeling. It was obvious that by working separately in both analytical and global modes, and then bringing them both together, Dan had improved his overall performance remarkably.

Since that time I have often suggested to my students that they notice during their practice whether they have a tendency to emphasize either the global or the analytical approach. Most of them have told me that raising this question allowed them to evaluate their approach more objectively, and that they have been able to work on building up those qualities that were lacking in their performance as a result.

Exercise: Balancing the two approaches

VOCALISE

Slowly

S. Rachmaninoff

(Voice)　　　　la la la　etc.

Softly/expressively

1. Play or sing Rachmaninoff's 'Vocalise'.
2. Now repeat the piece using the 'analytical' approach. Observe the rhythms, dynamic markings, crescendos and

diminuendos exactly. Play the piece with the execution of a highly trained robot, without attempting to put any feeling or expression into the music.

3. Play or sing the same piece using the 'global' approach. Let your rhythm be flexible; use accelerando and ritardando whenever it feels appropriate; focus on the quality of your tone and vibrato, and the expression of feeling. Play the piece with spontaneity, and respond to any insights that come your way.

4. Now play or sing the piece again with an awareness of both analytical precision (accuracy in detail and rhythm) and global understanding (warmth and flexibility). Allow your attention to move naturally between analytical and global functions. Be aware of what is happening, but don't attempt to force one style on the other.

How was this time different from each of the others? Did you feel that the last time you played the piece you glimpsed or achieved a more complete or integrated interpretation than when you played it the first time?

5. Repeat the four-step process with a piece of your own choice. What did you learn from each stage of the process?

6. When you listen to solo or chamber performers, notice whether they are tending to emphasize the technical and analytical or the global and expressive aspect of their performance. How does their playing affect you?

Balancing when one approach predominates

Have you noticed, either from the previous exercise or from your answers to the preference test, that you tend to favour one of the two approaches we have been discussing? Several of my students asked me how they could become more versatile in working with both approaches. Many of them found they possessed adequate skills in both areas, but that they were less likely actually to use the skills in one area than the other. But all of them felt that by exploring the side they were less inclined toward, they could round out their overall skills and musicianship.

If you tend to favour the *analytical* approach, you can make a point of emphasizing the global side of yourself during your practice for a day, a week, or more. Here are some suggestions:

1. If you normally keep a journal or goal notebook for practising, give your journal a break for this period.

2. When you have played a piece, respond only to your feelings, intuitions and physical insights.

3. Let your practice time pass without monitoring a watch or clock. Forget about time, and practise until you feel you have accomplished enough for the day rather than until a given time period is up.

4. Do *not* use a metronome or any other time-beating device while practising. Notice whether you learn as well this way as you do when you're using a metronome.

5. Be creative with the music; set yourself positive experience goals for your practice and give yourself room to play and enjoy.

6. Experiment with imagery to enhance your sense of the feeling and meaning of what you are playing. Practise the techniques of letting go.

7. If you make mistakes while you're practising, simply continue with your playing without stopping to correct every last detail.

8. Explore new fingerings for difficult-seeming passages.

9. Allow yourself to follow the interests and explorations of the moment; don't feel obliged to limit yourself to the goals you have set for yourself, but allow yourself to develop new musical goals as you go along.

If you tend to favour the *global* approach, you can make a point of emphasizing your analytical side during your practice for a day, a week or more. Here are some suggestions:

1. Set yourself specific goals (see Chap. 5, p. 83), list them, and cross each item off your list when you've accomplished it.

2. Plan the order of your practice session, beginning with the simplest tasks and progressing to more complex ones.

3. Set yourself a specific time limit for accomplishing each goal.

4. Observe the proper rhythm, pitch, articulations, fingerings, bowings and dynamics.

5. Use a metronome and tape recorder to help you analyse

your playing and control inaccuracies. Increase the setting on your metronome gradually until you are at full tempo.

6. If you make a mistake, stop and correct your error before moving on.

7. Play in a logical and orderly manner, and be aware of how each bar fits into the complete structure of the piece.

8. Maintain a critical and analytical attitude to what goes on during your practice session, noticing the order and efficiency with which you do things.

The greatest musical personalities of our times appear to defy all preferences for one approach over the other. Maestros Giulini, Solti and Kubelik, and performers such as Itzhak Perlman, James Galway and Placido Domingo, appear to be equally versatile with both approaches. They bring a blend of the scholarly and the intuitive, the formal and the expressive, the analytical and the global to their playing. But are they necessarily trying to keep these opposing qualities in exact balance at all times?

It isn't that simple. Some kinds of music – Baroque, Classical, and certain types of contemporary music – require a treatment that is predominantly analytical. The music needs to be precise, orderly and disciplined. The great performers and conductors understand this and respect it, while also bringing their emotional and intuitive side into play.

On the other hand, late Classical, Romantic and some twentieth-century music, as well as some of the slower Baroque movements, can be most effectively performed with a predominantly global and expressive approach. This music needs to communicate feelings and complex emotions, and calls for a more flexible and intuitive approach. Once again, the great musicians sense this, and play Brahms rather differently from the way they play Bach.

Some composers, such as Mozart, Beethoven and Mahler, can often be interpreted either way, in styles ranging from the analytical and intellectual to the global and intuitive – and still sound wonderful.

It's simply not possible to lay down hard and fast rules about this kind of thing, and even if it were, performance styles would still change over the years. But becoming flexible in the uses and strengths of both approaches, the analytical and the global, allows us to 'mix our own palette' in response to different pieces and to find a new and appropriate balance with each performance.

14 Ensemble playing

One of the questions I'm frequently asked when I conduct Inner Game workshops has to do with playing in ensembles and groups. 'I can see how the Inner Game can be applied to teaching and learning an instrument,' my friends tell me, 'but what does it have to offer the ensemble player?'

When I was in high school, second-period band and fourth-period orchestra rehearsals were the highlights of the day. I felt pride in knowing that I was playing my part in the massive sound of eighty musicians working together. I was fascinated by the unique sound qualities of the different groups of instruments – the strings, wind, brass and percussion.

Our ensemble prepared for weeks before each public concert, and finally the evening would arrive. The auditorium would fill with our parents, our brothers, sisters and teachers; the house lights would go down, the curtain would rise, and we would make music. The power and beauty of so many people working together as a team was audibly real. We could feel the music reaching and moving the audience.

Many musicians remember their first few years of ensemble playing with special affection; but after years of ensemble playing they say that something seems to happen, and much of the excitement goes out of the process. They begin to feel bored at rehearsals that would have delighted them a few years before. Instead of enjoying their brief solos and taking pleasure in playing a supporting role during the bulk of a piece, they wish they had a more impressive part to play. Instead of accepting the conductor as a co-worker who is shaping the overall musical interpretation of the piece, they begin to perceive him as a taskmaster. The music hasn't changed – but a quite wonderful experience has somehow deteriorated.

Of course, this is a generalization, and there are always musicians in any ensemble who still feel that original excitement and fulfillment. Musicians of all ages have musical experiences ranging from the profound to the problematic. And yet, for too many of us, something important has undoubtedly changed and a certain magic has been lost.

Those who feel unhappy often attribute their problems to a loss of personal identity or to boredom. Perhaps we find it difficult to hear ourselves in a larger group. Perhaps we feel that we can have but little musical impact on the larger sound. Perhaps long familiarity with ensemble playing has simply led to our taking for granted something that previously inspired and delighted us. What does the Inner Game approach have to say about this? Can we use it to revitalize our experience of ensemble playing?

Applying the insights of the Inner Game to ensemble playing involves the use of the Inner Game skills of will, trust and awareness.

The *will* skill of goal clarity is important in setting yourself new performance, experience and learning goals that are appropriate when you are playing with a large group of individuals.

When you have established these goals, the Inner Game skills of trust and awareness come into play. By *trusting* your own training and ability, you will find you can play without becoming distracted by 'peer group' concerns about the opinions other players have of you.

By expanding your *awareness* of the music so that it encompasses not only your own playing, but that of other sections of the ensemble, and of the entire orchestra or choir, you can deepen your own playing, your ability to make music harmoniously with others and your overall experience of the music itself.

Will Skills: The need for goal clarity

Playing in a jazz ensemble, band or orchestra or singing in a choir involves a number of factors that can lead to Self 1 having a field day. As an ensemble player, you must be responsive to the musicians around you in matters of pitch and rhythm, and yield yourself to the musical taste, tempos, styles and interpretations of the conductor, choir director or bandleader. It's only natural that you feel much less in control of your music than you do when you're playing yourself.

Self 1 doesn't appreciate being out of control of things, as we saw in Chapter 6. You may feel that everyone is telling you what to do – from your stand partners to the section leaders, and from the administration to the conductor – and that your opportunity for individual expression as a musician is getting lost in the shuffle. And yet your contribution is important: you are part of a team, and a team whose members lose interest becomes weak and uninspiring.

That's why it's important for you to set yourselves fresh goals in the areas of performance, experience and learning – so that your interest returns, and you once again feel yourself to be part of the larger whole – playing music that no one individual could possibly play, and taking delight in it.

Experience goals in ensemble playing

When you play with others, your musical experience is bound to be different. Some of the delights of individual performance are no longer available to you, but there are opportunities for enjoyment in ensemble playing that can more than compensate for them.

Not everyone enjoys the pressures and burdens of solo playing, of being 'front and centre' all the time. Many of us can actually experience relief and satisfaction when we are able to let go to the leadership and authority of a competent director. As a member of a larger group, we may feel freer to express our musicianship without self-consciousness than we would if our individual playing were spotlighted.

What kinds of experience goals can you look for when playing with others? You can experience and enjoy the way that your own playing blends in with that of your own section. You can enjoy the feeling of mixing, blending, belonging and flowing together with the other players. You can share a sense of energy with them that is not possible when you're playing solo. You can experience all this with your colleagues in your own section – and even more with the whole ensemble.

And you can make a lot more sound! For me, one of the great thrills of playing in a fine group is the excitement of co-ordinating my playing with that of others, playing together with anywhere from three to a hundred other musicians as if we were one.

In the final analysis, it's the sense of being a part of the symphonic work, the great choral work or 'big band' sound that everything else builds up to – and it can be a tremendous musical experience.

Performance goals in ensemble playing

The ensemble player faces a variety of different challenges at the performance level, and this variety offers us a clue to the possibilities for new performance goals. At times, a violinist may play a short solo; moments later he may be dividing a part with another violinist on the same stand; then they may find themselves blending in with the sound of the entire string section or balancing the sound of the strings with that of the wind section. You may be asked to play the melody, a countermelody, an accompaniment figure to a woodwind solo, or a supporting rhythm.

As we have seen, the ensemble player's Self 1 must constantly yield control to the directions and cues of others. The conductor will largely determine the tempo and style in which a piece is performed and will control balances and textures. Your pitch may need to be determined by the players around you: flute and clarinet need to be in tune with each other, and the brass players have to make similar adjustments within their section. Nor can Self 1 take full control of your entrances. It may tell you to wait for the wind section to reach bar 237, but the conductor may have you enter with the baton instead.

All in all, there are no clear-cut 'rights and wrongs' to ensemble playing; each member of the team responds flexibly to each fresh situation, each new demand. You will want your performance goals to reflect the variety of demands that are made on you as an ensemble musician and to tailor them to your specific circumstances.

Learning goals in ensemble playing

Most of my own experience in adapting the Inner Game to music has come from my ensemble playing. This is where I practise my Inner Game skills. I find that the communications from conductor to musician offer me many opportunities to practise translating 'do this' instructions into awareness pointers, and I am constantly learning more about how to coach others in ways that encourage rather than intimidate them.

When fifty to a hundred people work together to create a musical experience, there are unlimited opportunities for human interaction – large musical groups are extended 'learning labs' for every brand of mental interference, external and internal. In a group setting I can observe the ways in which I respond to my own doubts and fears and how I manage peer group pressure and other outside distractions. One can learn a great deal about co-operation through playing or singing with others, and I sometimes wish the world's political leaders would spend a week or two working together in an orchestra or choir.

Finally, playing in a group gives me opportunities to learn something about the magnificent musical literature for ensembles and to share in some of the greatest masterworks ever written.

Trust skills in ensemble playing

There are three areas in ensemble playing where your trust can be expressed – or withheld.

●   You can trust (or doubt) your own ability to play your own part.

In Chapter 6, we saw how doubt, fear and an excessive

wish to be 'in control' can block your trust in your own playing. Part of the trust involved in ensemble playing is trust in yourself.

● There can be trust (or doubt) between you and your fellow players.

When it's time for you to make an entrance and your partner isn't ready for it, you may begin to doubt whether you're in the right place. How can you play your best when the members of your section are all playing with a slightly different feeling for the rhythm? How can you handle the times when they seem not to trust you? And how can you express your trust in them?

You can use your trust skills to deal with any situation where the opinions of colleagues or other authorities would otherwise distress and distract you – whether the distraction comes from your section leader, the union, the management or the board of directors.

● Finally, trust can be instilled by or withheld from the conductor.

Some conductors can draw the best out of their musicians, while others sow confusion, guilt, and doubt. Eugenia Zukerman, in her novel *Deceptive Cadence* describes the antics of George Szell, the great conductor of the Cleveland Orchestra. Szell was a conductor of the old school, who would virtually whip his musicians into form.

Soloist Lynn Harrell, who was principal cellist with the Cleveland Orchestra under Maestro Szell for eight years, recalls that he was humiliated, threatened and once even socked in the back by the maestro. 'Szell was from that European generation of music directors who had total power,' he said; and added, 'It is possible to have authority without tyranny.'

Times have changed in the past twenty years, and there is now a much wider agreement that an atmosphere of trust is more productive than an atmosphere of threats and doubt. Many contemporary conductors have found ways of encouraging that sense of trust in the players under their baton.

Max Rudolf: disciplinarian and scholar

Max Rudolf, who was music director of the Cincinnati Symphony from 1958 to 1970 and formerly a conductor at the Metropolitan Opera, is known as one of the great scholars of the podium. His immense knowledge of the lives and background of the composers whose work he conducts, of the different performing styles, of history and psychology, have all contributed to his effective leadership.

In his rehearsals Rudolf doesn't simply tell his player how he wants them to play a given phrase; he also explains the historical reasons why he wants it played that way. By the time the concert comes around, his musicians have gained confidence in the authenticity of his interpretation and performance style, and Rudolf then concerns himself with the music rather than with individual performers. This allows the musicians in turn to stay in touch with their own parts and the wider context of the piece as a whole, instead of succumbing to doubt and anxiety.

Gunther Schuller: leaving room for mistakes and magic

The contemporary composer and conductor Gunther Schuller used to play the French horn in an orchestra. The horn is one of the hardest instruments to master, and Schuller knows better than most the problems an ensemble player can face. As a result, he is sympathetic when his players encounter difficulties.

Schuller believes in creating an atmosphere where it's OK to miss a note. He encourages his musicians to respond spontaneously to the music and doesn't seek to control every last detail. As a result, his players feel relaxed and are able to concentrate more fully on their playing.

Schuller likes to rehearse a passage thoroughly, but stop a little short of perfection. He explained to me that rather than feel obliged to try to duplicate under the pressure of performance what they have achieved in rehearsal, he wants to leave room for his musicians to 'rise to the occasion' in the actual performance.

215

James Levine: instilling trust through sheer love of music

James Levine communicates most effectively when he shows the musicians who are playing under his baton his joy in music. He rarely stops smiling. Rather than instructing a musician how to play a given phrase, he describes the sound qualities and the emotional expression he is looking for, and thus creates a musical experience for the performer.

It is very difficult to be nervous and concerned about the mechanics of playing while Levine is beaming from ear to ear, and as a result musicians give their best when they play with him.

Leonard Bernstein: an overpowering personality

Leonard Bernstein sweeps you up with his gestures. He's a dynamic and energetic conductor, and musicians respond to the powerful way in which he communicates his feeling for the music.

I recall playing in a concert in Carnegie Hall, with Bernstein conducting the Cincinnati Symphony and André Watts performing Brahms' First Piano Concerto. Bernstein's infectious enthusiasm (and unfocused eyes) convinced orchestral players and audience alike that they were witnessing some kind of privileged communication between Bernstein and Brahms.

It's as though Bernstein somehow becomes the pure energy of the music he conducts. And his own sense of being caught up in the music communicates itself to his musicians, who find themselves also caught up in his inspiration and able to let go to his direction.

Awareness Skills

Each of these legendary contemporary conductors manages to draw the best out of the musicians who play with them. Each of them manages this by setting up a communication between conductor and musician that allows the players to perform with a minimum of Self 1 interference. The key in each case is their ability to focus on the area of awareness.

Not all conductors, however, have mastered the skill of communicating a trusting atmosphere to their performers. I like to think I can play my best regardless of who is on the podium and what they may say to the musicians, but there have been times when a conductor's well-meant comments have nevertheless triggered a fury of Self 1 doubts and anxieties inside me, which in turn has severely blocked my ability to make music.

At the Music Educators National Conference in San Antonio, Tim Gallwey and I introduced the Inner Game approach to hundreds of music teachers. Immediately following our presentation, I found myself invited to rehearse with a string orchestra composed of teachers and students from throughout the United States. The majority of the musicians were string teachers rather than professional players, and we were directed by a distinguished conductor who had formerly been a violinist with the Philadelphia Orchestra.

We were rehearsing a demanding work by a contemporary composer, and quite frankly, the ensemble was struggling with the piece. I, meanwhile, was still on cloud nine after the Inner Game presentation, and when the conductor turned to my section and said, 'Yuk! You basses sound like a herd of elephants – you're too loud,' my heart sank about six feet. On the one hand, I wanted to crawl under the floor, I was so embarrassed. On the other, I was furious at the obvious comparison of the double bass, an instrument I love, with the largest animal in the zoo.

Next, our conductor attacked the violin section. He accused them of sloppy playing and told them the viola section played twice as well as they did. Trust was at a low ebb.

I felt insulted and wanted to walk out there and then. I muttered to myself that the real elephant was the one trampling around up there on the podium. Why should I tolerate this kind of verbal abuse? The rehearsal was ruined for me; the sense of musical companionship with the others that I'd felt after the presentation was gone. I couldn't concentrate on my own playing, the section I was with, the music itself, or even the conductor's beat.

Perhaps my reaction was a little extreme, but I think this story is an important one, because it illustrates how easily a conductor's casual comment can trigger feelings that seriously inhibit the musicians he is supposed to be leading. When a conductor's comments aren't directed at what needs to be heard, felt, seen, or understood, they can cause interference and negative reactions.

On occasions like these, the conductor functions as a kind of Self 1 to the 'body' of the orchestra. When Self 1's doubts and fears occupy our attention, the body tenses up and we are unable to play at our best. When we trust the body and our inner potential, on the other hand, we play without interference – and a conductor who functions as Self 2, sharing his awareness and trust with the body of the orchestra, naturally brings out the best in his players.

Like a coach or parent, the conductor can create a calm and trusting atmosphere by translating 'do' instructions into focuses for the musicians' awareness. Ensemble musicians, if necessary, can quietly make this translation for themselves.

About awareness instructions

As we have seen, instructions that include the word 'try' imply the possibility of success or failure and thus encourage tension and doubt. Awareness instructions are doubt free, they contain no implicit judgements, and they are simple to follow.

I once played under conductor Jorge Mester and was delighted to notice the way in which his handling of a difficult passage for cello in rehearsal managed to sidestep 'trying' and doubt. The cellist was unable to shift quickly to a high note without sounding tense and out of tune. Maestro Mester asked the cellist not to worry about accuracy of pitch, but instead to watch him smile and to smile back as she shifted to the note. His instruction served two purposes: it removed any pressure the cellist thought she was under to 'get it right', and at the same time allowed her to relax. The result was that her body relaxed and she was able to execute the shift perfectly, with warm tone and exact pitch.

Keeping your instructions simple, suggesting a specific focus for the player's awareness, avoiding judgements and 'do this' and 'try' instructions, finding imaginative ways to sidestrack Self 1 and creating trust are the keys to success.

Conductors who can translate their 'do this' or 'try' instructions into awareness instructions can do much to help their musicians stay in balance. Musicians who can locate the focus of awareness that's usually hiding inside a 'do this' instruction – and sidestep the rest – will be able to play as if the conductor were giving them awareness instructions.

Let's take a look at a few examples. Suppose a conductor gives the 'do this' instruction 'Basses, you are playing much too loud. Play softer.' Musicians who receive this instruction can choose to locate the focus of awareness in the words 'loud' and 'softer', and pay closer attention to their volume. Or the conductor who is on the point of giving this instruction might rephrase it in his head as an awareness instruction and say instead, 'Basses, notice whether your volume is too loud for the cellos still to come through.'

This second instruction gives each bass player a responsibility to listen to his or her own volume and that of the cellos. Thus if one bass is playing too loud and another too soft, both of them can adjust their playing to the point where cellos and basses are balanced.

'Violins, your pizzicatos are not together. Let's get it right,' is a 'do this' instruction. The equivalent awareness instruction might be 'Violins, listen to see whether you are behind or ahead of the other violins with your pizzicato,' or 'Listen to the melody in the oboe, and play your pizzicato with her as she changes notes.' Since each musician is now listening for the same clue, and playing accordingly, the section as a whole will play together.

Another 'do' and 'try' instruction might be 'Flute section, you are playing flat. Let's try to keep this in tune.' An equivalent awareness instruction might be 'Flutes, listen to the pitch of the clarinet in the preceding bar and notice if you're in tune with it.' This contains no value judgement, doesn't suggest *trying*, and focuses the flautist's awareness simply and directly on the pitch of another instrument. The flautist thus receives enough feedback to make any adjustment in pitch that is needed.

Again, 'Brass, you are too early with your entrance. Come in later this time,' could be rephrased as an awareness instruction: 'Brass, notice whether you are early or late with your entrance,' or 'Pay attention to the three notes in the violins just before you come in.' The first alternative invites each section member to take individual responsibility for the timing of the entrance, while the second adds goal clarity and increases each musician's awareness of the context in which the entrance is made.

A technique for increasing awareness

Frankly, I used to feel bored much of the time while I was playing in the symphony: the bass part is often very simple. I would also sometimes feel impatient with the conductor for spending so much time with more prominent sections of the orchestra. Then I'd get frustrated at my own mistakes, particularly when I'd play what I thought was correct, but find I was out of tune or dragging behind compared with the rest of the orchestra. I didn't understand at the time that the conductor's comments to other sections could be of value to me and my own playing.

Recently, I have found that increasing my awareness of other aspects of rehearsals besides my own part has greatly increased my enjoyment of ensemble playing. I have learned that what the conductor says to the violins does indeed affect me, and this adds to my sense of participation.

When I play my own part, I listen to myself as a member of a team of eight basses and communicate with the rest of the section with my own body language and by using peripheral vision to keep track of them.

I've learned to listen to the sound of the rest of the orchestra and to balance the sound of our section with it. This helps me to change my tone when appropriate in order to blend in with the cellos in one passage or play percussively to match the sounds of the tympani in another.

Sometimes section players can stay in closer step with their colleagues by listening to instruments that are carrying the rhythm below the melody, such as the French horns, violas or cellos.

I enjoy using my sense of feeling when there are no visual or sound cues to guide me. There are times when I must trust and let go to my hands to come in on cue. While I'm watching the conductor's beat, I notice which part of the music the conductor is focusing on; the character of the beat may be suited to the woodwind and inappropriate for the double bass. Sometimes the conductor won't cue the basses for an entrance, and then my awareness of the other instruments can guide me.

Playing together

One of the hardest things to do in an ensemble is to play together. I have found it very helpful to focus on another voice, whether I'm playing the melody, a countermelody or an accompaniment figure. I find it is natural when I'm playing a secondary part to let my mind 'sing along' with the main melody.

When you're playing the melody, you can make up a duet with yourself. When another instrument is playing a part that relates naturally to your own, you can 'internalize' their part while playing yours. You don't have to memorize the other part to do this; just allow your inner voice to ride the line, and sense how it fits in with your own part.

This technique increases your awareness of the rhythm, volume, tone, counterpoints and harmonies of the entire piece. It helps you play along with others in tune and with accurate rhythm, and it also makes you feel more a part of the overall musical effect. I don't feel as isolated and overwhelmed in larger ensembles as I used to, and I find that orchestral playing can be as challenging and exciting as playing in a chamber ensemble of five or six players.

I encourage you to experiment with 'singing along' in your next ensemble rehearsal and to notice any difference in your own awareness and how this can affect your playing.

Exercise: Playing together

When you are playing or singing in an ensemble, allow yourself to sing along in this way with another part. You will find this increases your musical feedback and that you will be able to play your own part with more accuracy, sensitivity, and meaning than before.

Let's take an example from this excerpt from Beethoven's Fifth Symphony, second movement, *Andante con moto*. Since you can't be all the instruments in a string section at one time, you'll need to grasp the general principles from this example and then apply them in real rehearsals with your ensemble.

SYMPHONY No. 5

1. Suppose you're playing the cello part. In the beginning you play the melody in unison with the violas. Sing the melody as you play, and see whether you're with the rest of the section.

2. Repeat the exercise, this time playing the melody and singing along with the bass pizzicato. Does this affect your rhythmic accuracy? Does it enhance your understanding of the harmony?

3. Now imagine you are the basses playing pizzicato. Sing the melody in the violas and cellos to yourself as you play the bass rhythm. When you sing the first two pickup notes to yourself, is it easier for you to know when to play your downbeat? How does singing the demi-semi-quavers in the melody affect the way you phrase the quavers? Does following the melody create any overall phrasing for your pizzicato? Do you notice any subtle changes in the dynamics when you follow the melody in this way?

4. Now look at the second phrase of the Beethoven:

5. If you play the cello line (viola, cello and bass together), sing along with the violins who are carrying the melody.

6. Notice your ability to play together with the other instruments in your section after you sing the three violin notes that precede your entrance.

7. In the second bar, can you feel all the instruments playing together on the downbeat after the semi-quaver pickups in the preceding bar?

8. Pay attention to your volume, so that you can still hear and follow the melody over your own part.

9. Does your awareness that all the instruments are moving into a crescendo together affect the volume at which

you play? Notice whether your crescendo covers up the melody.

10. How does the information you receive by singing along with another part in your head relate to the cues you're receiving from the conductor? Are the conductor's cues more meaningful and relevant to your part?

Here are some other awareness exercises that can help you integrate your sound into that of the ensemble. Notice how your sight, sound, feeling and understanding can increase your feedback from other parts of the ensemble and thus help you in your own interpretation and performance.

Exercise: Visual awareness

1. Notice which musical voices (melody, inner voice, rhythm, countermelody, bass line, etc.) the conductor is gesturing towards.

2. Watch and notice how the conductor's facial expression, hands, body and baton reflect the meaning the conductor wants to draw from the particular voice he's conducting.

3. Notice how the bow directions, bow placement, articulations, and attacks reflect the sound quality and the intensity of the music.

4. Watch the physical movements of the other members of your section as they prepare for an entrance.

5. With your eyes a little out of focus, see how many different aspects of the performance you can watch without focusing on one particular object. Your music? Yourself, your posture and handling of your instrument? The conductor? The performance space? The stand? The colleagues in your own section?

6. Notice when your visual attention is drawn specifically to one of these areas.

Exercise: Sound awareness

1. Listen for the ways in which your part reflects the meaning, nuances, colours, character and other emotional and expressive elements in the music.

2. Hear how your instrument is blending in with the person next to you, with the section as a whole, and with the other instruments who are playing the same or related parts.

3. Notice the blend, volume, contrast and rhythmic interplay of any two voices (bass and tenor, soprano and second soprano, rhythm and melody, etc.).

4. Sing along (in your head) with a part that complements your own.

5. Be aware of the pitch of the other instruments that are closest to your own range. Follow the intervals created by the two voices – the octaves, thirds, unisons, dissonances and consonances.

6. Listen for the voice that has the closest rhythmic interplay with your own. Notice if you are playing with these instruments or if your pulse is ahead of or behind them.

7. Notice whether your attacks and releases are ahead of, with or behind the rest of your section.

8. When you're playing an accompaniment figure, play at a volume that still allows you to hear the more important voices in another part of the orchestra. (In the Beethoven example given earlier, the basses would play at a piano level so they could still hear the violas and cellos carrying the melody.

Exercise: Feeling awareness

1. Notice any feelings of resistance or tension in your hands, arms, body or voice as you play or sing.

2. Since you cannot always hear other voices that are playing similar parts to your own, examine how much feedback your body can give you with regard to pitch and rhythmic accuracy, and the balance and meaning of the music.

3. Notice the feelings that are expressed in the music by your instrument, the other voices, and the entire ensemble.

4. Notice how these feelings are reflected in your own body as you perform. Where in your body do you feel the different emotions and musical vibrations?

Exercise: Knowing awareness

1. Pay attention to the personal background of the composer, the history of the work, and the time in which the piece was writen. How can you reflect this knowledge in your own playing?

2. Let your awareness of the form, style and construction of the piece illuminate the significance of your own part. How does your part fit into the introduction? Into thematic statements? The development? Recaps? The coda? The ending?

3. Notice the meaning of the specific sounds in your part and the way in which your part relates to the complete texture in terms of emotional quality, story line, static sounds, transitional material, etc.

4. Be aware of the function your particular voice has in relationship to the texture of the music as a whole. Are you playing the melody, the rhythm, an inner voice? What does your voice add to the texture and colour?

You can select from among these exercises, or invent your own means of focusing your awareness on your own part, the parts that interact with yours, and the entire ensemble. These exercises will help you to feel more fully involved in your playing in larger and smaller groups, add colour and precision to your performance, add to your experience and enjoyment of the music you are playing, and, hopefully, bring back some more of that musical magic that can turn ensemble playing from something you take for granted into a challenge and a delight.

15 Improvisation, composition and creativity

I have always admired jazz musicians for their ability to improvise. Playing some music that's written in a score is one thing, but weaving variations and improvisations 'out of thin air' is quite another. The early classical musicians were often masters of improvisation too; Bach was famous for his ability to improvise a fugue on a selected subject, and the cadenzas in some classical concertos were originally intended to be improvised, although written cadenzas are now usually played instead. The essence of improvisation is to play a spontaneous composition of one's own that 'fits' the underlying form – whether that be a sixteen-bar blues or the melody and structure of Beethoven's Emperor Concerto.

Jazz players acknowledge that they can improvise 'faster' than they can play from the printed page; in other words, a player can create an improvisation in the moment that they would find it hard to play with equal speed, fluency and musicality if it was somehow written down and set before them on the printed page. Improvisation is a form of 'kissing the Joy as it flies', to use William Blake's famous phrase.

Improvisation demands a real 'letting go' to Self 2. The fact that when improvising it is possible to play passages of a complexity and musicality that would be hard to master from the written page suggests something of Self 2's extraordinary power.

Improvisation puts us in touch with music that comes from within us rather than from the mind of a composer as expressed on the printed page, and shows that each one of us is capable of drawing music from inside us. Improvising is a kind of instantaneous composition.

I have found that when I experience and develop my ability to improvise, I strengthen my connection with my own musicality and can bring an increased spontaneity and freshness to my performance of written music.

As I mentioned in Chapter 1, my brother Jerry had cerebral palsy from birth. He has used the piano as a 'biofeedback tool' to improve his motor co-ordination in the fingers of his left hand. The sound of the piano tells him what his fingers are doing, and this feedback allows him to understand more about what his fingers are up to.

Jerry's experiments with body awareness and music inspired me to invite Fancon Shur, a creative improvisatory dancer, to co-teach one of my classes. Each of my students in turn had an opportunity to improvise music, while the other students did improvisatory movement exercises under Ms. Shur's direction.

Elizabeth played unaccompanied cello. She began by playing the prelude from a Bach suite. The music had a flowing melodic line of semi-quavers and interesting harmonies, but after several minutes Liz felt she needed to change pace. She started to weave variations and improvisations around Bach's themes and noticed that the class responded by transforming her sounds into new shapes and movements.

Liz began to experiment a little more: she played faster and slower, higher and lower; happily, romantically and sadly; and observed the ways in which the dancers responded to every change in her mood. Then she slipped out of Bach's style completely and began to play entirely from her own feelings, improvising with different rhythms and harmonic structures. She explained later that she had 'played without thinking' and let the music flow from her moment-to-moment sense of discovery.

Finally, Elizabeth returned to the more formal style of Bach, and brought the piece to a conclusion: she had intuitively structured the whole piece, giving it a formal beginning, a free-form 'second movement', and a conclusion that recapitulated her opening.

Those of us who were dancing had a marvellous time. We felt our bodies responding powerfully to Elizabeth's playing and were able to 'let go' with our bodies to the movements that suggested themselves. Liz told us afterwards that she'd never improvised before and that she had touched areas of feeling and emotion in her playing that went far deeper than her usual experience of playing written music.

Exercise: Discovering your own music

My brother developed this exercise as a way of working with his own body awareness to discover the music within him. It's a simple way to slip into the experience of improvisation and composition.

1. Sit at the piano. Allow your hands and arms to hang loosely from your shoulders, and breathe in a free and natural manner. Notice the position of your head in relation to your back.

2. Rock back and forth on your pelvis. As you breathe, allow your sense of weight to transfer itself from your pelvis into your hands. Keep rocking back and forth with the pelvis as you begin to play or sing.

3. Play or sing one single note as you rock back and forth.

4. Play several other notes, and be aware of your breathing and any tension in your body. Does the sound change as your body feels more tense or more relaxed? Can the tone of the notes reflect your mood (happy, sad, romantic, playful)?

5. Begin to combine notes at different tempos. Play intervals on the keyboard. Notice the feeling of the sounds created when you combine two or three notes.

6. As you play more intervals, with different note lengths, volume and sound quality, follow your impulses. Let the sense of music within you direct your playing. Do you notice any shaping of rhythm, melody, texture or colour emerging as you play?

7. Begin to experiment with longer spontaneous phrases. Notice how the sounds reflect your inner feelings.

8. Take a theme or fragment of a piece you are familiar with and allow your own ideas and improvised variations to emerge from it.

9. Use visual imagery to stimulate your imagination:

imagine different scenes, colours and atmospheres, and let your playing express them.

10. Allow your fingers or voice to speak for your body rather than your mind.

11. Experiment with formal structures. Start with one musical idea and allow it to grow, then play a section that contrasts with the first idea, and then return to the original idea for a concluding section: this gives you an A B A structure. You can also explore other forms, such as A B A B A, A B C B A, and A B C D.

What did you learn from this experiment? Did you come in contact with your own inner music? Did you notice yourself playing with freedom, with contrasting expression, with subtle control?

12. Now play a practice piece of your choice. Does your playing sound any different after your recent experience with exploring your inner music? Were you able to bring some of your spontaneity to this printed piece?

Discovering the composer within you

Most musicians at one time or another have dreamed of composing a song, a symphony or the sound track for a movie, but many of us feel that it takes a special talent to compose. Improvisation, and exercises like the one above, show us that everyone has some ability to discover music inside himself. Even if you've never done so before, you might like to explore the composer within you.

The exercises that follow will allow you to explore your inner composer by starting with an external idea such as *sadness*, internalizing it, and then externalizing it again as a physical response that takes the form of musical expression.

You can play your usual instrument if you feel technically comfortable and feel you can play without worrying about fingering and notes, or you can use your voice to sing, hum or vocalize in the scat style, or you can play at a keyboard. I'd suggest you use a keyboard if that will help you to dissociate yourself from preconceived ideas about what you can and can't do on your own instrument.

As you play, keep in mind that

1. there's no need to play fast;

2. it's OK to use any part of your body (elbows, arms, hands, etc.) and that your hand position doesn't have to be 'correct';

3. it's OK if you play out of tune;

4. it's best to perform these exercises in complete privacy.

Keep your ideas short and simple. Refrain from judging the music you make as good or bad. You don't have to like everything you play as long as you pay attention to your experience of playing. If you notice yourself 'trying hard', return to a simpler task.

Exercise 1: Sadness

SADNESS

Imagine the face of someone who is feeling sad. How do you feel when you're sad? Breathe in, and as you exhale, close your eyes and imagine a feeling of sadness washing through you. Perhaps you can sense a tightening of your chest and throat. Imagine there's a heavy weight on your heart.

As the sadness begins to fill you, allow it to express itself through your body. Begin to play notes that convey your sense of sadness.

Notice which intervals and combinations of notes best express your feeling of sadness. Listen to your playing and allow your sadness to create its own sound and mood.

Exercise 2: Blues

You're probably familiar with the 'St Louis Blues':

ST. LOUIS BLUES

W. C. Handy

231

Imagine yourself playing the melody in a lazy, carefree spirit. Now hum or play the melody and allow your sense of the blues to express itself. Notice the triplet rhythm of the music, and as you're humming or playing, begin to leave the melody while still keeping this rhythm. If you're playing a keyboard instrument, let your fingers rest on C, E, F, F sharp and G. You can add E flat and B flat if you want to. Let your fingers explore these notes in any order or combination, however your body sense or intuition suggests.

Exercise 3: Anger

Imagine you have a very formal and easily angered music teacher. Every time you play a few notes of a scale, your teacher interrupts you, screams at you, and tells you to stop. Close your eyes, and imagine your response to your teacher: let yourself feel angry.

Feel the emotions inside you; then give them physical expression on your instrument or in your singing. You may want to explore sounds that shout or wail, high or low pitches, clusters of discordant notes.

Let your playing explore the possibilities of expressing these emotions more forcefully. Notice how you translate your emotions into musical form and which sounds work best to express your feelings.

Exercise 4: A bouncing ball

Imagine the ball in a table tennis match, bouncing back and forth from one side of the net to the other. Let the notes C and G represent the moments when it hits the paddle on one side, then the other. Being to play along with your imaginary game, ping (C) . . . pong (G) . . . ping . . . When you find you're playing with an even tempo, imagine the match speeding up. Let it get fast and furious, and match the rapid exchanges and slams with your own playing of those two notes. Pick up the pace of the notes . . . and let them slow down again.

Exercise 5: Integrating what you've learned

As you read the story below, let your body respond to the words and express the various feelings of sadness, the blues, anger and so on in sound. Play as much or as little as you like, but only play the music that you feel welling up inside you. Don't think about what you're doing, just let go to your feelings and your body.

Bill was a young kid who loved to play the *blues* on the piano . . . (begin to play in the style of the 'St Louis Blues') . . . But his teacher wouldn't let him play that kind of music during his lessons. He made him play *scales* instead . . . (shift to playing scales) . . . When he missed a note, his teacher would *angrily* interrupt his scales . . . (anger theme alternating with scales) . . .

After Bill's lesson, he went around to a friend's house for a game of table tennis. He let his pent up *anger* and frustration out at he *hit* the ball across the table . . . (ball motif) . . . Finally, he made one last *slam* and won the match . . .

At home that evening he sat at the piano and began to play his favourite *blues* . . . (blues melody in the right hand) . . . But the memory of the *table tennis* came back to him . . . (left hand playing supporting chords with the ping-pong dynamic) . . . As the power and energy he'd felt during the ping-pong game moved through him, the blues too became stronger and more powerful . . .

Did you find you were able to express a variety of emotions and feelings in music? Were you able to combine the steady rhythm of the table tennis match with the melody of the blues? Did you find that improvising music came more easily to you when you were associating the music with your imagined feelings?

Did you notice yourself judging your playing as you went along? If you found the instructions for the exercise difficult to follow, repeat the exercise, this time just playing what comes naturally to you. Were any parts of the exercise particularly frustrating for you? Do you know why? Were any parts particularly enjoyable? Did you have fun? Did you learn anything about your ability to find music within you?

Trusting your sense of music

The part of us that hums, whistles, improvises and composes music is natural and unselfconscious, and it is the same natural and intuitive sense that the great performers tap into when they are playing music.

Soprano Martina Arroyo told me that when she is going on stage to sing the title role in *Aida* and her mind tells her 'You're going to forget the words', she has learned to ask her 'gut' to show her what to do. She pointed to her stomach and said, '*This* is where I can feel what is right.' André Watts once told me that when he is at a loss for how to play a phrase, what fingering to use, or exactly when to play a chord, he gets his answers from an 'inner feeling'. He told me that when he ignores what 'feels best' and does 'what his mind tells him to do', he is always disappointed at the result.

It's very hard to put into words this sense that your body has a different way of knowing from your mind, but whether you call it 'intuition' or a 'gut response' or an 'inner feeling', the musical sense that comes from the core of your being has the whole power of Self 2 behind it.

I've found that I can only stay receptive to my body's sense of 'knowing-feeling' when I maintain a calm and level physical awareness. If I begin to scurry around, worrying whether I have got everything under control, I lose touch with that inner sense. You may be familiar with the hectic sense that you've 'got to do this . . . don't have time for that . . . mustn't forget to keep the fingers curved and play the right dynamic . . .' This pressured feeling is a reliable clue to the fact that your body awareness is blocked and that you've lost contact with your intuitive, deeper sense of music.

When you can return to a calm and relaxed state, you may find that your unresolved problems have a way of receiving unsolicited solutions – without all that mental anguish.

Tapping into relaxation

Many people find that one excellent way to deepen their experience of relaxation and develop visualization skills is through the use of 'relaxation tapes'. The tape script that follows is designed to lead you through three processes: a 'progressive muscular relaxation' of the body; a 'meditation' or quieting of the mind; and a 'visualization' of yourself 're-creating' the music you play with the help of your deep inner resources.

I suggest that you make a tape of yourself or a friend reading this script. You can then use the tape to prepare yourself in the weeks and days before a performance. But you will also find that the format is very easy to learn. After using it a few times you should be able to close your eyes and run through a shortened version of any of the three parts of the formula (plus introduction and lead out) 'in your head' with no difficulty. This will allow you to relax and prepare yourself in any circumstance where you have ten minutes or thirty minutes in which to close your eyes and practise the technique.

You should record your tape of this script in a quiet place. You may want to ask a friend with a gentle reading voice to record it for you. The script should be read slowly, in a quiet, warm tone of voice, with a few seconds pause signalled by ellipsis points (. . .), and longer pauses at the end of each paragraph. An average page of script should probably take about five minutes to record, and the whole tape should run for perhaps thirty minutes.

Introduction
Find a place where you can sit or lie down in comfort, and where you will not be disturbed for the next half an hour. Find a comfortable position for your body. You can sit in a chair with your feet flat on the floor, or sit on the floor with your legs crossed and hands on your thighs, or even lie down (but not if you think you're likely to fall asleep). Loosen any tight clothing so that you can breathe deeply and comfortably. As you hear the instructions to breathe in and out, let your breath find its own natural rhythm. The idea isn't to match your breathing to the timing of the words on the tape; it's simply to remain aware of your breathing as you relax . . .

Progressive muscular relaxation
Close your eyes . . . You are breathing gently in and out . . .

235

slowly in . . . and out . . . Let your breath slowly flow in and fill you . . . and flow out . . . As you breathe deeply in . . . and out . . . let your worries and thoughts drift away . . . and relax . . .

Now pay attention to your calves . . . Feel your calves . . . Slowly tighten the muscles in your calves . . . and hold *it* . . . and let go . . . Feel the tension melting away . . . Your calf muscles feel relaxed, heavy and warm . . .

Breathe in deeply, and relax . . .

Now bring your attention to your thighs . . . Feel your legs . . . Slowly tighten the muscles . . . and hold *it* . . . and let go . . . As you feel the tension melting away, your legs feel relaxed, heavy and warm . . .

Breathe in deeply, and relax . . .

Take another slow, deep breath, and let your worries drift away . . . Let your breath flow gently in . . . and out . . .

Now bring your attention to your pelvis . . . Feel your pelvis. . . . Slowly tighten your pelvic muscles . . . and hold *it* . . . and let go . . .

Let your breath move in . . . and out . . . and relax . . .

Pay attention to your stomach area . . . Feel the muscles . . . tense them . . . hold *it* . . . and let go . . .

Breathe in deeply, and relax . . .

Bring your attention to the chest area . . . Feel any tension in your chest as you breathe slowly in . . . and out . . . Tense the muscles . . . hold *it* . . . and let go . . . As you breathe in, notice any remaining tension in your chest . . . and as you breathe out . . . let go . . .

Breathe in . . . and out . . . and relax . . .

Pay attention to your arms and hands . . . Feel your arms . . . Slowly tighten the muscles in your arms and hands . . . and hold *it* . . . and let go . . . Feel the tension melting away . . . Your arms and hands feel relaxed, heavy, and warm . . .

Breathe in deeply, and relax . . .

Now bring your attention to your neck and shoulders . . . Feel the muscles in the neck and shoulders . . . tense them . . . hold *it* . . . and let go . . .

Breathe in . . . and out . . . and relax . . .

Now bring your attention to your forehead, and the muscles around your eyes, and your jaw muscles . . . Tense the muscles in your forehead . . . and around your eyes . . . and in your jaw . . . and hold *it* . . . and let go . . .

Breathe in . . . and out . . . and relax . . .

Scan your whole body, and if you feel any tension anywhere, let it go . . . Your whole body is relaxed . . . and heavy . . . and warm . . .

You feel calm, and relaxed, and at peace . . . Enjoy this warm and relaxed feeling . . . Notice how soft your muscles are . . . Whenever you feel tense, you can return to this refreshing, calm state of deep relaxation . . .

Breathe in . . . and out . . . and relax . . .

Breath awareness
Breathe in . . . and out . . . and let go . . .

Allow your thoughts to drift away like bubbles . . . and bring your attention back to your breathing . . .

Breathe gently in . . . and out . . .

In . . . and out . . .

Follow the flow of your breath as it comes deeply in . . . and fills you . . . and flows gently out . . .

Just be aware of your breathing . . .

Let go of your worries and concerns, and follow your breath as it flows in . . . and out . . .

Breathe gently in . . . and out . . .

In . . . and out . . .

Follow the flow of your breath as it comes in . . . and fills you . . . and flows out . . .

Be aware of your breathing . . .

Breathe gently in . . . and out . . .

In . . . and out . . .

Let your thoughts drift away . . . and bring your attention back to your breathing . . .

Breathe in . . . and out . . .

Follow the flow of your breath as it comes deeply in . . . and fills you . . . and flows gently out . . .

Just be aware of your breathing . . .

In . . . and out . . .

Follow your breath as it flows in . . . and out . . .

Breathe gently in . . . and out . . .

In . . . and out . . .

Follow the flow of your breath as it comes in . . . and fills you . . . and flows out . . .

Be aware of your breathing . . .

Breathe gently in . . . and out . . .

In . . . and out . . .

No thoughts, no worries . . .

Breathing in . . .

And out . . .

In . . .

And out . . .

Deeply in . . .

And out . . .

Flowing gently along like a river . . .

In . . . and out . . .

So peaceful . . .

In . . . and out . . .

Breathe in . . . and out . . .

Your whole body feels relaxed . . .

And calm . . .

And at peace . . .

Take one more deep breath in . . .

And let go . . .

And relax . . .

Visualization

Breathe in . . . and out . . . and relax . . .

In . . . and out . . .

Let go of your worries, and breathe in . . . and out . . . and relax . . .

Bring your thoughts quietly to today . . . to this hour . . . to these moments . . .

Breathe gently in . . . and out . . . and let go . . .

As your breath flows gently in and out, imagine yourself calm . . . and relaxed . . . and at peace . . .

See yourself calm . . . and relaxed . . . and ready for the performance . . .

Breathe deeply in . . . and let go . . .

See yourself ready to go onstage . . . calm . . . and relaxed . . . and ready . . .

Breathe in . . . and let go . . .

Feel yourself in touch with your inner energy and strength . . .

Breathe in . . . and let go . . .

Watch your breath flowing in and out . . . and imagine yourself taking your position on stage . . . relaxed . . . and confident . . . knowing everything you have learned is inside you . . . in touch with yourself . . . with your sense of music . . . with your love of music . . .

Your breath is your energy . . . calm . . . and deep . . . as you breathe in . . . and out . . .

See yourself calmly playing the opening phrase . . . with a deep and confident feeling . . . hearing the sound of your musical voice . . . flowing . . . connecting you with the music . . .

Breathing in . . . and out . . .

See yourself playing your music . . . making music . . . hear the music . . .

You are relaxed . . . and alert . . . and at peace . . .

Breathing in . . . and out . . .

You are expressing . . . flowing with the music . . . becoming the music . . .

Breathing softly in . . . and out . . .

Breathing in . . . and out . . .

Your whole body . . . the music . . .

Breathing in . . . and out . . .

Your feelings . . . the music . . .

Breathing in . . . and out . . .

Your breath . . . the music . . .

Breathing in . . . and out . . .

Moving through the different pieces . . . Your body responding to the different pieces . . . Your breath . . . In . . . and out . . .

Breathing in . . . and out . . .

You are expressing . . . flowing with the music . . . becoming the music . . .

See yourself playing your music . . . making music . . . hear the music . . .

You are relaxed . . . at one with the music . . . at peace . . .

Breathing in . . . and out . . .

Breathe deeply in . . .

And out . . .
And relax . . .

Lead out
You are calm . . . and prepared . . . and alert . . .
Take one more breath, and slowly open your eyes . . .
Feel your body . . . calm and relaxed . . . feel your energy
. . . your sense of purpose . . . your love of music . . .
Begin to move your body, slowly at first . . .
Your arms are loose and flexible . . . your back, neck and
shoulders comfortable . . . your legs relaxed . . .
Stand up and gently stretch your whole body . . .
Breathe in . . . and feel any tension in your body . . . and let
go . . .

Trusting your intuition

I was playing outdoors with my children one sum-
mer's day and lost all track of the time. I suddenly realized I
needed to rush off to a symphony concert. I had one of those
small and easily ignored hunches that I'd better not forget
anything this time, because I wouldn't have time to go back if
I left anything behind – but I was too frantic to pay any
attention to it.

I arrived at my locker as the five-minute buzzer sounded.
As I rushed into my trousers, shirt and coat, I looked down at
my feet and realized I was in big trouble. I'd been wearing
white athletic socks with my running shoes and hadn't
brought any black socks with me. That's a *disaster*! I play my
bass on a high stool at the very edge of the stage, and my
whiter than white socks would be extremely visible.

The locker room was almost empty, as most of the musicians had already left for the stage. I panicked. And then
another hint came. Something told me to go into the adjacent
rehearsal room. I opened the door and went in – nothing but
chairs and music stands.

Then I noticed the double doors leading to the furnace
room. Again, that inner sense prompted me to look inside. I
could hear the rest of the orchestra warming up, and I told
myself there was no logical reason for looking for black socks

in the boiler room – but once again, I followed my intuitive prompting.

I burst through the double doors and noticed a closed toolbox next to the boilers. My inner feelings told me to open the box – and *voilá, eureka, lo and behold*: three-inch *black* duct tape.

As I heard the orchestra tuning to the A, I taped my ankles, ran to the stage entrance, walked casually onstage, and took my place in the nick of time.

Don't ask me to explain these things, but it does seem that we know more than we sometimes realize. Music is a creative and intuitive art, and what we learn about creativity and intuition by playing the Inner Game of Music can be very helpful in playing the Inner Game of Life. If you like, I 'improvised' a pair of black socks when there were no black socks to be found.

Dreams as a source of intuition

I have a story that illustrates the way in which intuition can work through dreams. This isn't too surprising, perhaps, since when we're dreaming, the parts of our 'knowing' that are unconscious can come to the fore and express themselves more freely than is always possible in the middle of a hectic waking life. Dreaming can give you insights and solutions to practical problems that you can use when you wake.

As I said at the beginning of this chapter, although I was trained as a classical bass player, I have always admired jazz bass players for their spontaneous improvisations and fluid technique. One night I dreamed I was playing 'My Funny Valentine' in a jazz style, accompanied by the great popular bass player Milton Hinton. I played with my 'bowed bass', and yet felt myself letting go to the freedom and joy of jazz improvision.

As soon as I woke up, I rushed to my instrument and played the music that was still fresh in my memory – and it was still there. I decided to call Milton Hinton, and asked him to play with me in one of my 'Green Machine' concerts. He accepted and we played together. It was a great experience.

My dream clearly taught me that I could play some of the jazz styles in my dream and this also gave me the inner direction to make this dream into reality.

After the performance, a student of mine told me, 'I'd never *dreamed* you could pull off a concert like that!' I had to laugh.

The gift of music

I've never found any limit to the surprises that are in store for us when we let go of our Self 1 concerns and listen to the promptings within us. And the great musicians are usually willing to credit a power greater than their everyday selves for the music that pours through them. Many of them regard it as a gift. As James McCracken expressed it to me once, 'Whatever I have to give is part of a much greater power for which I am just a conduit.'

Mozart knew this better than most, and I'd like to close this book with a passage from one of his letters that gives one a vivid sense of just how far that inner sense can go. He's describing the way in which he composes, and says that happens most naturally when he's travelling in a carriage or going for a stroll after a hearty meal. 'When or how my ideas come, I know not,' he writes, 'nor can I force them.'

He goes on to talk about the process of composition in more detail, and there's no other passage in the literature of music that so clearly expresses the wonder, profundity and joy that the gift of music can bring:

'Provided I am not disturbed,' he writes, 'my subject enlarges itself, becomes methodized and designed, and the whole, though it be long, stands almost complete and finished in my mind, so that I can survey it, like a fine picture or a beautiful statue, at a glance. Nor do I hear in my imagination the parts successively, but I hear them, as it were, all at once. What a delight this is I cannot tell!'

Mozart was certainly one of the great masters in the history of music, and one cannot perhaps expect revelations like this to happen all the time. Yet I firmly believe that we all have 'a touch of Mozart' within us, that there is indeed something truly marvellous inside each one of us, a potential that is all or more than we ever imagined.

Tim Gallwey has shown us that the more we rely on this true potential, the more it has to offer. Whether we play the Inner Game of Music or of Life, we learn that the answers to our questions lie within us.

Self 2 doesn't need approval or credit. It doesn't know anything about doubt or fear. It doesn't need to feel in control. It only wants to be – to enjoy – to experience – to play – and to be left alone.

When it has a chance to be heard, it stops all the clocks, surprises our inner and outer critics, surpasses our expectations and brings us pure pleasure. Let's give it a chance and enjoy its unfolding beauty.

Acknowledgements

All authors know how much they owe to others: family, friends, and teachers – the countless people behind the scenes who contributed time, energy, ideas, criticism, hints, interviews, encouragement and a thousand other shades of support. The acknowledgements page is an author's opportunity to thank and pay tribute to those many people without whom, as the saying rightly goes, the book could not have been written.

First, I'd like to thank Tim Gallwey: for answering the telephone that day in June 1980 and encouraging me to apply the techniques of the Inner Game to music. My thanks also for the years of friendship, the coaching and tennis lessons, and above all for your determination to make sure the Inner Game came across simply and clearly.

There are two others with whom I have worked in depth on this book, and I'd like to thank them both. Phyllis Rosser, I'm grateful to you for the skill with which you organized years of scrambled notes and anecdotes into the basis of the book; thanks for your patience, hospitality, sandwiches, encouragement, questions, clarifications, editing and a year of hard work. Charles Cameron, thank you for the gift of words; you put the finishing touches on the manuscript and gave it a hint of Mozart.

I would like to thank Mary Tarbell Green, my loving wife. Thank you, Mary, for withholding your approval from each chapter until you could understand every word. You mirrored every bad idea and good hunch right back at me, so that I could see which was which. You supported me when I

244

no longer thought I could see any light at the end of the tunnel. Thanks for keeping the kids busy when I needed to write. And most important of all, thanks for still loving me.

Thanks, Paul and Cindy Ellison, for teaching me to jog, and for your support from day one of a five-year marathon of friendship, professional help, spiritual growth and great canoe trips.

I'd also like to thank my brother, Jerry Green. Thanks, Jerry, for turning me on to the Inner Game of Skiing and setting this project in motion. Thanks, too, for the inspiration you have been to me, showing me how much is possible when you learn to let go.

Erika Andersen, thanks for taking me under your wing, and for being a guinea pig in my first Inner Game bass lesson. Special thanks for keeping the candle lit and making me throw out my first Inner Game article. Allen Imbarrato, your comments concerning Inner Game theory, simplicity, organization and exercises were very useful – but you could have let me score at least one game from you on the tennis court. Peggie Luey, I greatly appreciated the way you shared your talents as a Suzuki method teacher with me, and your invaluable suggestions for the 'Parent and Coach' chapter. Mike Hieber, your art workshops showed me that there are more than two sides to any problem. Kyril Magg, your woodwind suggestions were extremely helpful. John Leman, Janell Weinstock, Marcia Richardson, you brought the singers into this book. Thank you, Bob Schauer, for watching out for the brass players, and for your personal support of my writing and jogging. Nick Buscheff, your keyboard expertise and your help in class were invaluable. Mary Judge, the Cincinnati Symphony librarian, thank you for your copyright research and music editing. Simon Anderson, Professor of Music, thanks for your comments and suggestions about music listeners, and for encouraging me to remember the pop artists, rock musicians and jazz greats when I tended to get overly symphonic. Worth Gardner, you have given me the courage to plunge into music theatre your creative talents and our collaborations have inspired me to make a reality of my dreams.

Janos Starker, you have been a powerful force and have kept me from laziness. Harvey Phillips, I have been inspired by your energy and musical philosophy. André Watts, your generosity and artistry have taught me a lot about concentration. James McCracken, thanks again for lunch, your friendship, your belief in human potential, and your incredible singing. Martina Arroyo, my next book should be about your career; thanks for those wonderful, candid glimpses of moments in music. Yehudi Menuhin, my thanks for graciously sharing your insights as to what lies behind the finest musical performances. Maestros Michael Gielen, Bernard Rubenstein and Gunther Schuller, musicologist Phillip Crabtree, jazz musician and composer James Madara, French horn player Robin Graham, cellist Lynn Harrell, violinists Pinchas Zukerman and Kató Havas – your conversations have brought new insights, clarity, meaning and feeling to my life and to the Inner Game of Music. Thank you all so much.

In the beginning of any new venture, there are those who take personal, financial and professional risks to support an idea before it has become established. Some wonderful people sponsored workshops and demonstrations when I was first applying the Inner Game to music, and I owe them a debt of gratitude for their trust and support while the Inner Game of Music was still in its experimental stages.

Larry D. Snyder stuck his neck out by organizing the first five-day Inner Game of Music workshop in Akron, Ohio. Gail Berenson brought the Inner Game of Music to Ohio University in Athens, Ohio; Joshua Jacobson to Northeastern University in Boston; Lucas Drew to Miami, Florida, and the Music Educators National Conference in San Antonio; Eugene Gratovich to the Music Teachers' National Convention in Kansas City; Carlton Gushiken and Mark Kuraya to Hawaii; Bob Berg brought the Inner Game to New Zealand, Joan Wright to Australia, and Wei Boa-Zheng to China. My warmest thanks and appreciation to each of you.

I'd like to express my gratitude to the University of Cincinnati and the management of the Cincinnati Symphony for giving me the time off to conduct these workshops and write the book.

It was Judith Weber who convinced Doubleday to publish this book, and I thank her for it. I'd like to express my gratitude also to James Raimes, formerly with Doubleday, for his support of this project. And special thanks to my editors, Paul Aron, James Rosenthal and Patrick Filley, for their care in turning a manuscript into a book.

There are others too numerous to mention: my thanks to each one of you who saw something of interest in the works and took a chance to support and encourage it.

The Inner Game of Music has a home at the University of Cincinnati's College-Conservatory of Music. My thanks to Eugene Pridonoff for inviting me to teach the Inner Game seminars, which have served as an ongoing laboratory for the techniques and exercises described in this book, and to Warren George, who put together our summer workshops and special events. My bass students and the students in my Inner Game classes have been the willing volunteers in my sometimes crazy experiments. I'd like to thank my CCM students for walking in the door not knowing what to expect and being willing to try almost anything, and for creating, refining, practising and rediscovering what works and what doesn't. In a very special sense, you *are* this book.

If it were not for the encouragement that I received from friends, teachers and family during the early stages of my own musical education, I wouldn't have had the courage to pick up the phone and call Tim Gallwey.

Mom and Dad, you still gave me your love and support when I didn't choose to follow Dad in his sales business – and insisted that I attend the finest music school. I hope this book makes you proud.

Love and thanks to my sons Zach and Adam and stepson Richie for reminding me there is still a child inside each one of us that enjoys playing, learning and being free to express itself.

Abe Luboff, Murray Grodner, Henry Portnoi, Janos Starker, Fritz Magg, Joesph Gingold, David Baker, Jr, and Maestro Max Rudolf, each of you gave me encouragement at critical times when I was uncertain of my own abilities.

Maharaji, you showed me that the simplest way to find one's potential is to look within. My respectful thanks to each of you.

JULIA CAMERON

The Artist's Way

A Course in Discovering and Recovering Your Creative Self

Have you ever longed to be able to draw or paint, write or compose music? With *The Artist's Way* you can discover how to unlock your latent creativity and make your dreams a reality.

The Artist's Way provides a twelve-week course that guides you through the process of recovering your creative self. It dispels the 'I'm not talented enough' conditioning that holds many people back and helps you to unleash your own inner artist. Its step-by-step approach enables you to:

- start your own path to creativity
- dissolve the barriers that are preventing your creativity impulse from finding yourself
- use your rediscovered talents in whatever way you wish
- learn that it is never too late to start fulfilling your dreams

'For those who will use them, these are powerful and effective tools for getting in touch with their own creativity'
Martin Scorsese

OTHER PAN BOOKS
AVAILABLE FROM PAN MACMILLAN

BARRY GREEN
THE MASTERY OF MUSIC   1 4050 0009 0   £9.99

W. TIMOTHY GALLWEY
THE INNER GAME OF GOLF   0 330 29512 8   £7.99

TONY BUZAN
MAKE THE MOST OF YOUR MIND   0 330 30262 0   £6.99

JULIA CAMERON
THE ARTIST'S WAY   0 330 34358 0   £12.99
GOD IS NO LAUGHING MATTER   0 330 48764 7   £6.99

All Pan Macmillan titles can be ordered from our website,
www.panmacmillan.com, or from your local bookshop
and are also available by post from:

Bookpost, PO Box 29, Douglas, Isle of Man IM99 1BQ
Credit cards accepted. For details:
Telephone: 01624 677237
Fax: 01624 670923
E-mail: bookshop@enterprise.net
www.bookpost.co.uk

Free postage and packing in the United Kingdom

Prices shown above were correct at the time of going to press.
Pan Macmillan reserve the right to show new retail prices on covers
which may differ from those previously advertised in the text
or elsewhere.